COUNTRY LIVING
IRISH COUNTRY STYLE

NICHOLAS MOSSE

COUNTRY LIVING

IRISH COUNTRY STYLE

NICHOLAS MOSSE

DECORATING WITH POTTERY, FABRIC, AND FURNITURE

HEARST BOOKS
A DIVISION OF STERLING PUBLISHING CO., INC.
NEW YORK

10 9 8 7 6 5 4 3 2 1

Library of Congress Cataloging-in-Publication Data Available

Published by Hearst Books,
A Division of Sterling Publishing Co., Inc.
387 Park Avenue South, New York NY 10016

Originally published in hardcover by Hearst Books under the title *Irish Country*
© 1998 by Hearst Communications, Inc.

www.countryliving.com

Distributed in Canada by Sterling Publishing
c/o Canadian Manda Group, One Atlantic Avenue, Suite 105
Toronto, Ontario, Canada M6K 3E7

Distributed in Australia by Capricorn Link (Australia) Pty Ltd.
P.O. Box 704, Windsor, NSW 2756 Australia

Printed in China

ISBN 1-58816-238-9

CONTENTS

INTRODUCTION

Peace and radiant simplicity are what people seem to be looking for nowadays when they design their homes and work areas: a meditative interior for body as well as soul. We all know we cannot go back in time, we cannot relive our grandmother's life. But we can choose to treasure what grandmother has left to us, and keep the best of her lifestyle in our homes as well as our hearts. Here in Ireland the changes over the past thirty years have been so overwhelming that much has been swept aside, but there does exist a new and vibrant appreciation for traditional craft and custom, for Irish country style.

Before I begin, it might be worthwhile to explain briefly how Irish style evolved, which is really the story of how Irish country people lived their lives. Its very simplicity seems idyllic to us today, as there was so much more time for contact with other people, for talk and banter, than today's stressful life-style can provide. Imagine a life in the middle of green hayfields, steely blue skies, and stone walls stretching for miles. All your friends live just over the road and you see them every day; you share tasks, problems, joys. Your life revolves around the simple repetitive tasks of the country, when you use every object over and over again. Everything in your house speaks of the simple shapes of usefulness, made by hand, made to suit. There is not the slightest trace of pretension, not one false note. The constant demands of the countryside provide the inspiration for your life and how it is fashioned; the community fills each house with life and warmth and a bit of fun.

THE TRADITIONAL IRISH INTERIOR

The rural Irish dwelling was usually quite small, with a hearth-centred main area, which could be used for any purpose. The daily routine could be altered at a moment's notice: with a few chairs brought forward or a churn pushed back, the same room could provide space for a winter gathering of friends

OPPOSITE

*Simple and useful shapes.
The plain beauty of the
ploughed field or riverside
can also be found in
vernacular furniture and
everyday objects, such as
this famine chair, old linen
and spongeware pottery.*

7

BELOW

The ironwork of the countryside is a successful combination of the material with uncomplicated, pared-down forms.

and neighbours. Each item of furniture would be made locally and to order, as quirky as the notions of the owner. The slope of a meal bin or the size of a chair would be altered to fit the inhabitants. Big, pared-down shapes prevailed, as scarce materials and basic skills ensured limits to the housewife's imagination. Colours of whitewash and earth pigments were enriched by peat smoke and by touch. The stark ironwork utensils around the hearth were balanced by the colourful complexities of the Delft on the dresser and by the large, warm shapes of dairy crocks. Browns, blues, oxide red and all the colours of the landscape make up this special style, while the wonderful, relaxed cheeriness of an Irish cottage provide all the inspiration that is ever needed.

In my childhood, my parents would bring us on outings to the foothills of Wicklow, where I would plonk myself down on a brightly painted form or bench and listen to the stories and gossip issuing from our wonderful hostess Biddy. Biddy's house had everything – smooth round corners, a glorious hearth complete with three-legged pot and crane, a settle bed and the obligatory

dresser filled with colourful crockery. Its simplicity allowed room for the spirit to fly around a little, especially when the stories were particularly frightening. It was also amazingly flexible: the table was used to prepare food when placed lengthways along the wall, but when brought out into the room and dressed with a cloth, it instantly became a dining table. Nowadays, the space Biddy lived in would be considered suitable for a flat. This flat might have one bedroom, a bit of storage and a central living and working and dining area. I often think how clever we would all appear if we could live as simply and as flexibly as my old friend Biddy did.

In spite of the very basic minimalism of poverty, old cottages had an open, welcoming presence, yet you always knew whose house it was. The colour of the door, the horseshoe feature, or the carving on the settle bed were the individualistic touches that mirrored the inhabitants. Homemade and useful, the objects were cheerful as well. I do feel that handmade objects carry extra vibrations with them, they give you a different feel. I definitely prefer them

BELOW

In, on, through and around the countryside, animals are more plentiful than humans. This fine head belongs to my dog Odie.

and have found that once you start looking out for and using things made directly by hand, you get hooked. In my pottery, we do everything the hard way, or, as any industrialist would tell you, the wrong way. Because of this passion over handmade quality, I built up my workshop to make sure that everyone in it was spending time over an actual pot instead of a machine.

CONTEMPORARY CRAFTS

When I was little, my parents often had foreign designers visiting them while they worked at the national design education operation, Kilkenny Design Centre. This was started in 1965 and was conceived to improve and develop all areas of design in craft and industry, for the whole country. And while it lasted, a whole army of wonderful designers from Scandinavia and Europe spent long periods in the area. Some of them liked it so much they stayed.

Listening to these designers talk made me think that making things by hand was entirely possible as a way of living. I determined to be a potter from an early age and never wavered, going to Harrow College and studying with such potters as Mick Casson, Wally Keeler and Victor Margrie. After studying pottery in Japan, I came back home with a burning sense of tradition; the veneration the Japanese hold for their traditional crafts made me realize that it was a desirable way to go. I opened up my own workshop in a disused cow house and determined from the start to work in a traditional mode.

Over the years, I have trained local young people and have found enormous talent and painstaking craftsmanship in almost all of them. Many of them have developed into pure geniuses – a great thing to boast of in a small village. What they do is use their hands in a wonderful way and make things that differ ever so slightly in form or texture or touch of the brush. Indeed, these are the very differences that make up the cheerful, individualistic characteristics that are found in the best of Irish country style.

CHAPTER 1

INSPIRATIONS

For a small island, Ireland has the most wonderful, most enormous variety of geographical forms. Its landscape is an unending source of inspiration and venturing anywhere in the country is always a pleasure, never a bore. I often tell visiting friends that the landscape changes every twenty minutes from the window of a train or car. If you keep your eyes on the countryside, you can watch gentle hills give way to sand dunes, then panoramic mountains, and all in the space of an afternoon. A humble trip to the local village can still provide a feast for the eyes; long may it last!

Light and air must create the shimmering essence, the basic feel of any country. The turbulent, Gulf Stream skies of Ireland and the high latitude of the country provide a striking display of changing light that continues from every dawn to every dusk. When this slanting, wet light combines with the ever-changing landscape, unexpected beauties catch us unawares. It is this unpredictable beauty that pulls at the heartstrings of expatriate Irish. Perhaps because the Irish have lived hand-in-hand with their local landscape for so long, they have an intimacy with their particular region that is hard to find in other countries. No one has to work very hard to find natural, wild beauty. Many country dwellers can just open the back door and let in the view.

THE CHANGING COUNTRYSIDE

Most colours of the countryside are saturated with wetness. A tree in mist takes on a deep and dark aspect, which is most specifically Irish. Every colour is a bit heavier and so contrasts more strongly with its surroundings. A solitary tree in the middle of a hayfield could appear wispy and insubstantial in sunlight, then gloomy and velvety in a windy storm. This sense of atmosphere pervades the environment, toning down any sharp hues, and quieter colours look at home here. In our pottery, these are the colours we are always happy with – nature's colours moistened with a fine coat of mist.

The varying greys of Ireland are usually covered in lichens, making them appear softer and more beneficent. They are not cold and neutral; they are welcoming and touchable.

When you live in the middle of the countryside, detail is another feature of nature that insists on attention. Plants grow so quickly here that you can almost see the grass and little wild weeds growing and, every day, new inspection reveals surprising change, on the smallest levels. All these minute elements in a landscape affect our general perception of the big picture and mood of a place. They provide the real texture to the visual world. An Irish peat bog is a sweeping, open, almost empty-looking sort of place until you begin to examine it closely. You could liken it to an expanse of tweed; from afar it seems a solid colour, but poke your nose up to it, and you will see an amazing assortment of tiny coloured threads. A gentle wander through a bog will reveal tiny, cunning, entrancing plants and wee beasties. It will make anyone love the tiny things in life.

Stone of all type lies under and over the Irish landscape, often as a framework, sometimes as the central focus of the picture. It comes in all colours, depending on where you live in this small country, and you can find granite

stone walls changing to limestone in the same county. Any unquarried stone has a wonderful, soft, aged texture, no doubt because Ireland's landform and geology are so old and worn. Living in Kilkenny, I am surrounded by a fossil-filled black limestone called Kilkenny marble, a wonderfully workable stone. I also grew up with my mother's collection of old stone querns or grain mills and to me they are an example of Irish stone at its best. They have the hand-worked quality I love; the softness and the feeling of real life about them that I associate with Irish country style.

THE COLOURS OF IRELAND

The famous greens of Ireland are not just poetical or political imagination. They are so ever-present, they are almost like the air we breathe. Blue greens of winter barley, the yellowish greens of unfurling beech leaves, the blackish greens of thorn trees, have all been allowed to thrive because vast monoculture is not common here. Small farms are still worked and their patchworks of

Natural forms of the
landscape and natural
forms of material. The
colours and patterns of
nature are ever present in
Ireland. The swell of the
sea and the lushness of the
countryside mean that
nature is never far away –
an enduring, endearing and
continuous presence.

fields and hedges are a study in Irish green. I wonder if the pervasive greens of the countryside are not the motivation for country people's preference for bright and brilliant man-made hues. Traditionally, the small amount of timber used in Irish cottages was painted for protection. Originally, lead-based brown and green paints were used, but, in the nineteenth century, as more colourful, chemically complex dyes entered the marketplace, these colours became bolder and more amazing. Glorious pinks, lipstick reds, brilliant blues in high gloss paint were all over these cottages, replacing the earth-based colours of earlier times. Windows, window ledges, doors, the front gate and the bench outside were painted with gay abandon. They provided punctuation marks in the otherwise green landscape.

Soft is a word I could apply to all aspects of traditional Irish architecture, and it provides a sensual pleasure all of its own. The cosiness of a small Irish cottage is undeniable, not just in its size, but in the way it has been made. When something is made by hand, it is instantly obvious. A handmade brick is only a very distant relation to the machine-made bricks of today. The stones used for local cottages were not machine quarried in some distant area, they were local field stones that could be brought by horse and cart. The whitewash coating applied over the years further softened these cottages, with layer upon layer of wash building up into thick, crumbling blankets of lime covering the stone. Ochre, sienna, blue and a gentle pink used to be mixed with the white limewashes and, when used, these colours made sure that the cottages they covered nestled even more softly into the surrounding greens and greys.

TRADITIONAL MATERIALS

Natural materials were always the essential ingredients in traditional Irish crafts and first and foremost crafts were things of use. Sticks and straw and willow and ash and hazel have been used here from time immemorial. Straw

provided rope for a multitude of uses. I remember seeing my neighbours pulling a straw rope or sugan out of a stack of fresh hay; then, with only two people and a long iron hook, they magically produced material for covering chair seats or for tying up almost anything. The soft golden colour and tactility of the material belies its toughness. Sugan chairs are wooden framed but with seats woven of straw; they last a very long time indeed.

The branches of the hedgerow provided the Irish with utilitarian wares as well. Willow or hazel baskets are lightweight and beautiful and were made here for innumerable purposes. My brother has a collection of old fishing creels, but potato steamers, cradles, hampers and turf-carrying containers were also common. A willow basket will make anything look better and will provide that anything with a bit of ventilation as well. The shapes of these vessels were strong and dictated by the material.

In building work, hedgerow material's flexibility allowed traditional craftsmen to create curving hearths in a house, by bending a wicker frame

and fixing it with daub and plaster. Wicker has its own geometry, a natural tendency to bend a particular way, to great visual effect. Again, that softness that Ireland is so good at. A very particular form of flat rush matting on floors was very common as well and the soft greeny gold colour must have been a comfortable presence.

All the best things have survived the test of time in Ireland. Although much harder to find and now created for a whole new world and market, you can still find rural artefacts being made all over the country. Nowadays, they are luxury items, but the charm of the maker's hand is still there and it is wonderful to know that certain traditional crafts continue to be passed down from generation to generation. Willow baskets from Galway, rushwork from County Laois, amazing tweeds from Donegal, weaving from Kerry, linens from the north, together with handknits, stone and ironwork: all of these crafts are very healthy industries nowadays and I hope that you will enjoy seeing some of my favourites in this book.

OPPOSITE AND BELOW
The daily rhythms of life in rural Ireland are in constant contact with the natural environment. Here fishing boats call in at the unspoiled little fishing village of Ballycotton, County Cork.

CHAPTER 2

POTTERY

The earth under our feet will provide. As Ireland sits on the furthest west side of the continent, the actual crafting skills enjoyed by mainland Europe never flourished here quite as well, although it is important to point out that the basic raw materials were to hand in various pockets throughout the island. One of my obsessions is with Irish clay, as the body of any pot is the most fundamental component. Clay will determine shape and strength and basic colouring and so pots made with Irish clay will differ from those made anywhere else. Different types of earth produce different types of pottery. Earthenware is clay that needs to be fired or cooked at relatively low temperatures, usually producing a red terracotta colour, but also to be found in yellow, brown and white body colours. Whiteware is white clay covered with a clear glaze, yellow ware is similar. If covered in a watered-down clay— or slip – it can be decorated by scratching or dribbling slips over the basic clay pot. Stoneware clays are different and they need to be fired at a higher temperature and fuse more completely, producing a more impermeable, less porous surface. Both these clays were used to create rough country pottery and are a far cry from porcelain, whose smooth, almost glasslike surface is used to produce the finest, most expensive wares. Recently, a good bit of research has been done into the history of early ceramics, and it is obvious that, throughout the years, small clay operations were set up in various areas, using local clay. Almost all of these have a connection with the story of Irish country style.

Neolithic pottery began with the smooth plainness of the leather it was made to replace. Decoration increased slowly and brown burnished vessels were becoming highly incised with cord and comb impressions by the late Bronze Age. These early pots would have been made by coiling long snakes of clay into cylinders, smoothing the surface out and then forming them into the desired shape. They would then have been incised with pointed tools to produce linear decorations and fired in stacks of wood to harden off the clay. The round-bottomed suspended pots from these early days must have looked like the little, black, round iron pots of today; their spherical shapes readily catch the flame of an open hearth and distribute the heat evenly to whatever is inside. Their strong simplicity and functional shapes foretell the future of pottery here. They could easily be mistaken for contemporary ceramics and would grace any table.

Although these ritual funerary pots and everyday ware were made in early times, the craft seems to have disappeared in Ireland during the first millennium A.D. It was the Vikings, and especially the Normans, who reintroduced clay pots to Ireland, and by the thirteenth century the potter's wheel was in use in some areas. A lump of wet clay coaxed into a shape on a centred and spinning horizontal wheel is much faster to fashion than the earlier coiled pots. Fired in flame, these early pots hardened sufficiently to last a good while.

In the absence of any strong pottery tradition, wooden vessels took the place of pottery for a long period of Irish history and this continued in poorer regions until the nineteenth century. In Dublin in the medieval era, there was an earthenware pottery known to us from written record; it was even on the 'Street of the Potters' now known as Mullinahack. In the seventeenth century, other records show plain and simple redware or terracotta being made in Dublin and Cork, so a market was obviously growing and efforts to service the market were being made. It is thought that Belfast was the first place to get a pottery factory up and running, as it can trace its roots back to 1688. For the most part, this Belfast ware aped the Delft being produced throughout the continent at the time – very chic and up to the minute, it was charming majolica-covered earthenware with beautiful brushwork, some of it blue and white, the best pieces multi-coloured. Majolica can be described as a heavy tin glaze of exceptional lustrous whiteness, which lends itself to decoration.

When applied to plain terracotta earthenware, the glaze coating totally covers the red base. Because this type of Delft is fired at the low temperatures of earthenware, the colours that are used for decoration maintain their vivacity and prettiness. I have actually had the privilege of examining the site of this early Belfast pottery with Peter Francis, a ceramic historian and archaeologist: standing on the quay in Belfast, I was fascinated by the thought of these early Irish potters and their tough life – finding and processing one's own clay is tough enough in this era of trucks, diggers and dumpers.

It is also fun to imagine the beginnings of trade at that time. Linen was taking off and being produced in sufficient quantities to fill ships bound for the colonies. A similar hustle and thrust must have been happening in ceramics, as the eighteenth-century records provide us with information about various small potteries up and down the country. The race was on to provide "import substitutions" and to keep ceramic wares from Rouen and Burgundy out of the country. Irish clay came into its own. Good supplies of different sorts of

clay body were located and mined, providing some happiness for a baby industry. Some of this clay was so good that it was exported. Tipperary clay went to Waterford by horse and cart, then to Holland by ship. Carrickfergus clay was sent over the water to Liverpool; Clonmel clay was exported, and Josiah Wedgwood in England imported clay from Tipperary and flint from Dublin to make his famous Queen's ware in the late eighteenth century. While he was importing Irish clay, he also made sure that the nascent Irish pottery stayed where it was, so as not to interfere with his own growing business.

The pots Mr Wedgwood and the famous eighteenth-century Irish potter Mr Delamain were making were, for the most part, for the wealthy only. But the need for good, strong, useful ceramics was still there and a few potteries took on that market. These items filled the needs of the day – town and country, pure and simple.

Where there was clay, the chances of a pottery taking root were increased. The nineteenth century saw the development of several small coarseware

OPPOSITE AND BELOW

Opposite are cream-separating pans. Milk was left to settle in these wide, flat pots and then the floating cream removed. In ceramics, no two white clay bodies are identical, as revealed in the small collection below of whiteware, earthenware, old creamware and stoneware.

potteries in outlying areas, mainly near clay deposits. Cork, Youghal, Monaghan, Coalisland, Castle Espie, Enniscorthy, Galway, Larne and Limerick can claim early pottery manufacturers, most of whom produced ware suitable for use in the country. The pottery made at this period for country usage would have been functional and cheap. For the most part, it would have revealed the clay it was made from, so redware or terracotta, yellow clays, brown glazed, and solid whitewares were the order of the day. It was honest stuff, handthrown for the most part and decorated simply, if at all. Shapes were perfectly utilitarian and more beautiful for it.

WHITEWARE

Whiteware, created for dairy and hygienic display in shops and butchers, is another type of coarse ware commonly found in the countryside. Although it was made from slipcasting techniques, its minimal, functional shapes carry that Irish feeling of use and worth. It is one of my favourite types of old pottery and over the years I have found pieces made in Belleek as well as in Dublin. Most of this whiteware would look stunning on the very latest, minimalist furniture, as its complementary shapes are strong and angular.

Made using a salt-glaze technique, storage bottles were also created in large numbers and in all shapes and volumes. Any old pub would have displayed salt-glazed or glazed brown, two-tone earthenware cylindrical bottles full of whiskey and often marked with the maker's name. The fact that so many of these items are still visible in antique shops supports the fact that they were made in vast quantities and served a growing economy well into the twentieth century. But the social and economic problems of the century took their toll and few of these country potteries lasted very long.

One exception is Paddy Murphy, a fifth-generation potter who carries on the tradition of redware much as his great-great-grandfather would have done

in 1835. Paddy lives near Enniscorthy at Hill View Pottery and produces planters and flowerpots in the old way and style. To me, he is a national living treasure and a bridge to the past history of Irish ceramics. He throws very simply and embellishes his surfaces with the time-honoured technique of incising the soft, unfired clay with stamped or routed designs and textures. The clay deposits around Enniscorthy have provided raw materials to Carley's Bridge pottery as well, where Paddy's grandfather got his training, and is also used by Kiltrea Bridge Pottery nowadays, for their range of red terracotta plants pots and kitchenware.

Opposite are piled antique coarse redware pots for planting outdoors. They are a perennial necessity. The utilitarian shapes of the brown saltglazed stoneware (left) flooded the Irish market and were used for all purposes – from cream or whiskey to liniment or ink.

Another blow to Ireland's original earthenware producers was the flood of imports arriving from the industrialized English potteries. The cheaper, heavier items continued to compete, but smaller, finer items found their way into the Irish countryside. Wares of white clay and strong colours were now affordable.

SPONGEWARE

Spongeware was a type of pottery specifically produced to appeal to the pocket and eye of country dwellers. To understand its charm for us today, perhaps a short explanation of how it was produced will assist. In ceramics, clay can be

Above are the felicitous

pair of birds who inspired

our plate project, shown on

pages 52-3.

The photograph opposite

shows the long-established

way to keep your porridge

warm and your tea

insulated. These pots are

all Irish, some marked with

a Belleek stamp on the

bottom, proving that the

grand old pottery for fine

porcelain also turned its

hand to humbler stuff.

made to do almost anything. The basic throwing of a pot on a wheel is fine for round shapes, but watering clay down into a state known as slip and then pouring this slip into plaster moulds can make more complex shapes. As the potteries of the west evolved, this complexity became ever more desirable. Plaster has been a part of European craftsmanship for hundreds of years and, as this technology grew, the ability to repeat a complex shape over and over and more and more cheaply grew as well. The early nineteenth century saw a proliferation of goods produced this way and it became possible to bang out vast quantities of 'biscuit' ware produced from plaster moulds. For many small potteries, crude, cheap items became their stock in trade, their bread and butter. As this inexpensive ware was held in scant regard, imperfections were part and parcel of the bottom-end pottery. Only low skill levels – perhaps apprentices who were probably untrained country people – were required to produce this early nineteenth-century ware.

Not only were the moulded shapes produced quickly and cheaply, the sponged decorations were as well. The use of sponges can be traced back a long way. In England, colour applied with sponges can be seen on late seventeenth- and early eighteenth-century fine ware; loose, schematic tree leaves are the commonest form of sponge decoration we can find at this time. But, some time around 1800, the trick of cutting the sponges occurred to someone on the shop floor and so, combined with delicate paintwork and expensive colours, cut sponge decoration emerged. Even Mr Wedgwood used this trick for his aristocratic ware and even he produced wild and wonderful designs. With the development of more reliable, artistic techniques, such as paper transfers from engraved plates, the use of sponges for fineware decoration fell off and was relegated to the back room during the early twentieth century.

No one is sure who started making the lowly ware we now call spongeware. Just as they do nowadays, potters copied other potters and travelled around

BELOW AND OPPOSITE

Dainty patterns or bold,
spongeware has always
come in many styles. A trip
to the local marketplace
offered a multitude from
which to choose. Indeed,
finding two identical
patterns would have been
a difficult task.

quite a bit. In my own mind, I feel it probably began in Staffordshire and travelled quickly up to Scotland, then over to Ireland. As so little value was placed on this production, the records and traces of it are dim indeed, but it is certain that Scottish potteries kept on producing it and that certain Irish workshops used the technique to bring in ready cash at a local level. Shards of broken bits of spongeware have been excavated from the Larne Pottery in County Antrim, which worked from around 1842 to 1857. Belleek Pottery, renowned for its high Victorian parian ware made from local Fermanagh clay (originally), found itself in sufficient trouble during the years around the First World War to have to make spongeware to ensure its survival.

SPONGEWARE SHAPES

Spongeware can be identified by shape as well as by decorative technique. Like other items destined for the countryside, it was functional in the extreme and the basic shapes which have come down to us are limited. Large mugs

and 'cans' (an antique term for tall, cylindrical, handled coffee mugs) were the commonest drinking shapes. The earliest examples had a beautifully hand-turned foot and added strap handle, often with some fancy detail on the bottom of the strap. These mugs would have provided tea in large quantities, generous and hospitable in the true country manner.

Bowls for individual use are also common shapes and were most likely used for the porridge or goody so frequently served. They were footed bowls with gentle curves, straightening outwards; in all parts of Ireland, they would have been displayed upside down – or whammelled – on a dresser shelf. Plates were used as well as platters, although the mug and bowl would have proved more useful to the daily diet of spud and 'stirabout'. Jugs came in all shapes and sizes, but from examples that remain extant today, it would appear that a pint and a quart size were most desirable. Jam was marketed for a period during the late nineteenth century in pint jugs – jam jugs – and these can still be found in antique shops.

BROWN JUG

For this glazed jug, we took our inspiration from a single-colour Victorian jug of similar size: straight sides are a bonus when sponging through a stencil. Copy the designs from page 135 onto prepared acetate using a felt-tipped pen. Then, on a cutting mat, carefully cut away the acetate with a craft knife where you want the design to show through, remembering to make little bridges for your stencil as you work.

MATERIALS

- *undecorated ceramic jug*
- *felt-tipped pen*
- *acetate*
- *Brown Jug templates (page 135)*
- *craft knife*
- *cutting mat*
- *water-based ceramic paints in white and black*
- *small pieces of sponge wound with insulation tape at one end to keep fingers clean*
- *white spirit for cleaning*
- *spray adhesive*

1 To create the pattern, work out the arrangement of the design elements and space them evenly around the pot. Make small marks with the felt-tipped pen.

2 Lightly mark the positions of the design by dotting through the acetate motif around the jug. To keep borders level and in line, use the top edge of the acetate as a line to measure against. If you make a mistake, it is easy to rectify with a wipe over the dots, then try again.

3 To prevent smearing the wet paint through the stencil, allow the paint to dry before applying a fresh motif. Here, we first sponged the border motif on every third set of dots. When the first set was dry, the adjacent motifs were stencilled, and then the remaining motifs. With a simple shape like this, you may be able to hold the acetate to the jug without a problem, but more complex motifs may need a coating of spray adhesive to keep all the small bits of the stencil in place. A little paint goes a long way, so do not pour out too much at a time. Dip your sponge into the paint and then test by dabbing away any excess on the side of your paint container or a spare plate or tile. Go for a light coating at the start, which you can build on with repeated dabs.

4 With all three borders done, begin the bands of floral motifs, sponging alternate flowers to prevent smearing. For this complex design use a quick spray of adhesive on the acetate so that you can concentrate on the detail when sponging. If you decide to change anything once the paint has dried, a quick scrape or wipe with white spirit should remove the offending bit.

Basins and ewers for washing are also found in spongeware patterns; on a pine washstand next to the quilt-covered iron bedstead, they must have added a cheerful note. Today, the ewers are rare birds indeed, as they must have suffered the indignities of daily travel none too well. Water carrying is something we need not worry about today, but used to take up hours of labour in days gone by. Little wonder that these large jugs have become so scarce.

Variation in basic shape took place slowly. As spongeware continued in Ireland until the 1950s, it is important to remember that the contemporary interior trends did eventually filter into this basic country ware. Shapes in the 1930s and later do reveal themselves as such and examination of technical points can also assist in dating these objects.

SPONGEWARE PATTERNS

What basic shapes lacked in the marketplace was more than compensated for by the plethora of available patterns. At one stage, when I began to look at old spongeware more closely, it occurred to me that there must have been as many patterns as there were decorators. The precise, perfectly repeated patterns of fine ware went out the window with spongeware and this very spontaneity and variety is a major part of its charm. We can perceive broad sweeps of regional pattern variation, but, because the wares were peddled by itinerant salesmen and because they were rarely marked with a maker's stamp, it is truly difficult to be certain about what was made by who, where, and for who.

Early Scottish spongeware seems to have combined brushwork with sponges from the beginning and this mixed technique was carried through for a long period, especially with the combination of cabbage roses and leaf forms, a particularly Scottish pattern. This sort of design links it to the ware being produced on the continent, in France and Holland. Another Scottish ware was derived from the Chinese design known as the Three Treasures.

OPPOSITE

A quintessential country friend. The crackled glaze of this piece signals venerable old age.

SHAMROCK BOWL

This design uses three small stencils and requires you to jigsaw two of them together to get the border nicely lined up. It is loosely based on an original Irish spongeware bowl from our own collection. In the old days, they also did this design in blue – so follow your own heart for colour preferences.

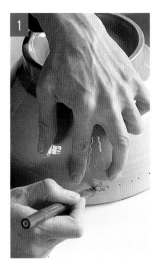

MATERIALS

- *undecorated ceramic bowl*
- *felt-tipped pen*
- *acetate*
- *craft knife*
- *cutting mat*
- *3 shamrock templates (page 138)*
- *water-based ceramic paints in brown and green*
- *small pieces of sponge prepared as on page 37*
- *white spirit for cleaning*

1 Copy the three designs onto acetate and make them into stencils as described on page 36. Using the width of the twig stencil, mark positional guides along the top border with tiny felt-tipped pen marks. Leave a small gap between each twig for each shamrock cluster. Keep the line of this border parallel with the top edge of the bowl by measuring or checking visually as you go.

2 Using the marks as guidance, sponge alternate twig motifs in brown around the rim. When dry, go back and finish by sponging the remaining twigs. Let the paint dry.

3 Take the shamrock cluster stencil and start sponging green onto the border, nudging the shamrocks right up to the twig motifs. Take your time, judging the position carefully before applying the paint. Also, take care that the clusters are all positioned at the same angle. Depending on the size of acetate you have used for your stencil, you may need to alternate paint dabbing. Let the paint dry, and then finish off the decor with the final green clusters.

4 Sprinkle the single shamrock stencil on the bottom section of the bowl. In this case, we have done a very loose sprinkle; you could have more or fewer shamrocks, as long as they are all equidistant. Each time you move the stencil, twist it by at least 45 degrees to retain the feeling of scattering. You also want the shamrocks to face in different directions. This is one instance where you will probably need to scrape off the occasional shamrock and retry. A light sprinkling of felt-tipped pen marks before starting painting would be helpful.

43

This pattern's development is a real study in how earlier design became derivative in the crudest way, when the bottom end of the market tried to imitate the top. Spongeware makers also tried to reproduce a very popular type of engraved paper transfer ware known as Syrian Pheasant, with amazing and amusing results. The childlike skills of these potters can be touching in the extreme.

It is often said that children were actually the decorators of spongeware. There is no way to confirm this, but it is safe to assume that, since sponging on decorative motifs required so little skill, children and women and unskilled labour were employed to create spongeware. (Newspaper advertisements at the time Belfast and Delamain potteries were in operation stated that they gave good work to 'distressed and foundling children'.) Certain motifs were more common than others, but how the motifs were combined and what colours were used seem to have been left to the imagination of the individual maker. For the most part, the colours employed were the standard, easily

obtainable colours of the period: strong browns, cobalt blues (light and dark), green, black and a dense red occasionally appearing as pink, provided the fundamental palette. These colours are not dissimilar to other hues found in Irish country dwellings and they sit happily together. The oxide paints of long ago have a similar feeling and mood. Other colours do appear and, when they do, they create collector's bloodlust for today's spongeware addicts.

Motifs were formed from sponge. There are many old wives' tales about the technique and I am not sure how old sponges would have been made. I do know that there were enormous numbers of different little pattern elements in circulation and they were combined in whimsical ways. Generally speaking, the little elements were dabbed on in a solid mode – one colour per dab – although the occasional larger sponge would have been loaded with several colours by the use of brushes. Stripes and brushwork appear a fair amount of the time, while stamped designs appear in combination with overall sponging only rarely. When this happens, a soft overall background sponged colour is

OPPOSITE AND BELOW

The strong geometric design featured opposite incorporates a vestigial tassel. Similarly, the leaf forms on the bowls below are anything but natural: the cutting of the sponge sets limits on fine detail. The repetitive use of the elements removes the 'leaves' still further from reality.

OPPOSITE

A group of spongeware

of varying styles can still

look comfortable together.

The beautiful Irish corner

cupboard – still with its

original scumbled paint

surface and wallpaper

background – is an

excellent example of the

best type of vernacular

furniture.

topped by differently hued, smaller cut sponge motifs. The scale of designs ranges from tiny wee dabs up to globular 5cm *(2in)* flowers and animals, but the scale is always in keeping with the piece and is always friendly to it.

Florals The old spongeware most often seen is floral, so even then, people held predilections for natural embellishment. Roses small, roses medium, roses large, roses barely looking like roses – these can all be found in various combinations. The small ones were smaller than your fingernail, while the big ones measure up to 7.5cm *(3in)*. Often with roses, a triplet of rose leaves in green was attached to the edge of the flower. Patterns of flowers were either centralized, banded, or scattered to the four winds and old patterns of roses were created in all these ways.

Daisy-style flowers were also popular, with a central radiating bunch of petals. The stylization of these types of flowers was strong and varying: petals could be blocky or perfect or slightly naturalistic. They could float, or they could nestle into leaf configurations, and they could be any colour whatsoever.

Leaves Put an ivy leaf with a rose or a daisy with a fern; it is all still very pretty. Several types of leaf motifs evolved over the long years. The main attribute of these designs was the cutting of the veins in the leaf to give a frilly, light feel with lots of energy. Fern leaves in particular were popular and are today a direct pointer to a Victorian obsession. In spongeware, they were used frequently and set up jaggedy patterns and rhythms when used in bands going around the pot. Smaller, solid leaves were often found in combination with linear stems, curling the same way over and over. Sometimes, precut 'garlands' drew scallops around edges, or encircled smaller motifs, such as flowers or birds. Seasonal holly leaves seem to have been produced at the turn of the century.

RIGHT

This bowl dates from the First World War, no doubt a gift or memento, primitive and touching.

Geometric Elements of geometry were also important in creating the built-up patterns of old spongeware. Diamond shapes were common: sometimes they were solid, sometimes cut internally into quarters or more elaborate geometric shapes. When run together or side by side, they would create the ever-appealing zigzag, apparently irresistible to an Irish country dweller.

Animals Animals are the hardest examples of early spongeware to find in today's antique shops. They were indeed made, however, and I have seen and loved cows, dogs, cogs (is it a cow or a dog?), birds (in pairs or singly), deer, roosters, butterflies, zebras and elephants. These last two are good examples of spongeware that was made to be sent to the colonies and beyond, from Africa to Indonesia. Why there are examples here in Ireland today is a mystery. Most animal motifs are the main element in a design, often placed centrally.

Commemorative Hard on the heels of exotic animals come the nationalist motifs. Shamrocks, the little Irish emblem, appear on old spongeware in several ways. One of the ones I like most is a wee, upside-down shamrock, regularly sprinkled over a mug; this design inspired an elegant Parisian shop to order a version of it from us as an exclusive. Occasional examples of shamrock mixed with harps are further proof of patriotic production. Aside from very simple shamrock bands, I know of only one other band of shamrock and this is a delicate, intricate garland of stem and three shamrocks.

COLLECTING SPONGEWARE

Whatever pieces of old spongeware are thrown together, they always look comfortable and right. Perhaps it is the scale or colour uniformity, but a medley of spongeware is always pretty. Irish countrywomen must have enjoyed it and minded it carefully, piling it up on their dressers. Plates were leaned forward against holding bars in many old dressers and the bowls were whammelled to keep out the dust and show the brightly coloured patterns to advantage. Mugs hung from hooks on upper shelves and platters took centre stage on the lower bottom shelf. We can do the same today and every year more people are bitten by the bug of spongeware collecting. Needless to say, every year it gets more and more expensive; however – that said – it is still within the range of ordinary mortals. Be sure to examine the piece carefully for damage: wear and tear is very much a part of this ware and is to be expected. My mother never bought cracked pieces, but I do with regular abandon. It is up to you to decide what standard of collecting to maintain. Some heavily restored pieces are coming onto the market now: you can usually tell restoration by surface texture or colour changes; it just is too good or doesn't feel right. As for what is treasured more, it is the old rule: the rarer, the dearer. Animals and insects are seen as more valuable than flowers. Complexity of design and whimsy also lend value, but if you like it, buy it. That is a sound rule.

Since we started in 1976, many other makers have come into existence. Most of these operate on an industrial scale such as well-known brands like Poole or Bridgwater. Many of these look quite modern, with large irregular motifs and colours to go with the latest trend, but recently smaller potteries have joined the fray and some of these produce very attractive wares. In the UK, look out for my sister Tania's designs for Brixton Pottery, which is run by her husband Alex Dufort. Even though the ware is industrially produced, her early Irish education and upbringing have obviously affected her charming designs. In the north of Ireland, there is Eden Pottery, which also finds inspiration in the animal world. No matter who creates spongeware, the look is so spontaneous that it is almost impossible not to create a fresh new look, one that is different from its neighbour. We definitely feel that when it is made by hand, start to finish, it carries an extra bonus with it.

BIRD PLATE

This simple design uses only two easily cut motifs. The bird motif is coloured with two tones while sponging, while the border is just a band of paint, lightly dabbed with natural sponge.

MATERIALS

- *undecorated ceramic plate*
- *felt-tipped pen*
- *acetate*
- *Bird templates (page 135)*
- *craft knife*
- *cutting mat*
- *spray adhesive (optional)*
- *water-based ceramic paints in red, blue and green*
- *small pieces of sponge, prepared as on page 37*
- *fine artist's brush*
- *natural sea sponge*
- *white spirit for cleaning*

1 Cut two stencils from the acetate as described on page 36: one of the singing birds and the second of the branches. Cut them on circular pieces of acetate as in the template on page 135. This will help centre the design on the plate or any other round piece. Carefully position the acetate featuring the bird motif on the plate and tape down or hold fast with some spray adhesive. To ensure the acetate is always in the right position, carefully draw around the edge with a felt-tipped pen before starting to paint.

2 First sponge the blue water-based ceramic paint carefully onto the top of the birds, leaving the bottom half clear for the red breasts. This second colour may be applied immediately, as long as you take care not to mix the paints. Pull away the acetate and allow the paint to dry. Then use the branch stencil, positioning it as for the birds. Apply the green paint and remove the acetate.

3 To finish this section, take a tiny brush and finish the 'bridges' with dabs of colour. Here, the open areas around the

head and neck and parts of the tail and wings need a little filling in. Leave the paint to dry and remove the felt-tipped guide line.

4 Finish the outer edge of the plate by taking the sea sponge and dipping it lightly into the green paint. Check to make sure the sponge isn't overloaded and do a preliminary test to get the feel of using quick light dabs to cover the surface. If you want a very open look, use the more open part of the sponge; for a tighter finish, use the smaller holes. It is best to use a free, fast, light touch.

CHAPTER 3

FABRICS

Think of what a piece of thread can do. A tiny, flexible and unending bit of fluff has certainly wrapped up a good bit of Ireland – and has joined it to the rest of the world several times over. For such a small island country, Ireland is incredibly famous for its exports of textiles and related goods, and it has been for a good while. Whether they are linen or tweed or Aran knits, Irish fabrics are instantly recognizable and a true synonym for quality. The story of how this came about is a complex one and has shaped the entire countryside over hundreds of years.

If you take a thread, you can create many types of article. With a single piece of yarn, you may crochet, knit, net or tat; you may create Jacob's ladders. With a bit of help from your feet, you may weave a crios (the traditional belt of the Aran islanders). With a loom, you can weave almost anything, depending on what your thread is made of. The two key ingredients to Ireland's textile history are the two indigenous base materials: one is the wool off the back of a sheep and one is the stem fibre of the flax plant. Both these materials have been available for hundreds of years and over those years the fortunes of those who used them have risen and fallen with the times. Both woollens and linens, however, began as home-based, self-sufficient industries and gradually evolved into the large industries they are now.

LINEN

Like any vernacular craft, the ways in which fabrics are woven and created differ from region to region. In 1272, there is an early reference to Irish linen being used ecclesiastically in Winchester on the far side of England, so the skills to produce excellent cloth were around at that early time. This very early cloth would have been about 56cm *(22in)* wide and produced for and under the auspices of the church. The northern European countries also slowly developed a trade in linen production, which developed into a strong business

*A famine chair, homespun
linen sheets and a
spongeware jug: when
combined, these sum up the
textures and feelings of Irish
country style. The chair was
my first purchase of Irish
country furniture and the
linen was rescued from a
convent in County Galway.*

by the seventeenth century. Ireland's part in this trade in the early days was confined to growing flax and creating spun thread, with enough surplus to export to Britain in the sixteenth century. Trade progressed, it grew, and the climate of Ireland was kind to the small-holding farmers who grew the flax plant in their suitable soil. An entire way of life, a whole area of endeavour was developed in the north of Ireland at this time and the business of linen grew and grew.

Before the Industrial Revolution, a countryside household would have been the main unit involved in the production of cloth. There are several steps in creating linen, beginning with planting the seed, pulling or harvesting the plants so that the entire stem is preserved and drying the harvest. When the small bundles of these stems – called beets – are dry, they are put into still ponds of water for over a week and then pulled out and dried once again. This process is called retting: it rots and softens the various parts of the flax stem so that the inner fibres can be removed from the outer stem. This removal is accomplished with much beating or scutching and is just one more physical task needing to be done. The inner fibres, once separated, have to be combed through pins to create fibres ready for spinning. In the early days, spinning took place at home, with the women spinning, children winding the resultant thread, and one or two looms being used by men. The work was difficult and shared by all, it had its own demanding time requirements and allowed little or no let up in the work. In the north, this way of life created a sense of independence and an affluence and pride which persists to this day.

Much of this early, home-based work received official patronage and promotion with various lords and gentlemen putting effort and money into the improvement of the linen trade. Much like the grant systems of the twentieth century, the seventeenth- and eighteenth-century governments' assistance made huge strides in creating the reputation that quality Irish linen deserves for

STENCILLED CURTAINS

These curtains are pure Irish. They are made from the simplest, plainest material made personal with stencilled motifs taken from old spongeware. They look spectacular and the time needed to make them is not as forbidding as you might think. A day of effort will give you fabric to die for. Once you have stencilled enough fabric, make up the curtains as you wish.

MATERIALS

- *2 prepared A4 sheets of acetate (see page 138)*
- *natural linen curtain fabric*
- *craft knife*
- *cutting mat*
- *plywood 70cm (28in) long and the width of the fabric plus 5cm (2in)*
- *PVC sheeting*
- *duct tape*
- *large drawing pins*
- *heavy thread*
- *set square*
- *double-sided tape*
- *fabric paints in blue and green*
- *prepared stencil sponges (see page 37)*
- *glass jars with lids*
- *cotton buds*

Preparation With the craft knife and cutting mat cut out the stencils from the acetate *(see page 138)*. Mark the top on each sheet. Cover the plywood with the PVC and tape at the back. Measure 5cm *(2in)* in from the sides of the board and apply the double-sided tape parallel to the edge. Repeat across the width. Lay the fabric selvages and top edge on top of the tape. Press down firmly. At the top of the board, push in a drawing pin 25mm *(1in)* in from the top and one side. With one of the stencils vertically placed, push in a second pin at

the base. Repeat, laying the sheet below this pin to locate a third one. Using the set square, repeat on the other side. Wind the thread tautly around the pins to make a grid.

1 Pin one A4 stencil at the top left-hand selvage and pin the second alongside. Cover the rest of the fabric with PVC. Make enough paints for all the fabric and keep in the jars.

2 Using a plate as a palette and rubber gloves, practise stencilling onto scrap fabric. Then print on the linen and leave to set for a minute.

3 Carefully lift the left-hand stencil and re-pin it next to the right-hand one, keeping it square with the top and side threads. Repeat with the right-hand stencil and stencil through both. Move across the width and when the first row is complete, move the stencils to the next marked line and work across the fabric as before. Continue to the foot of the fabric.

4 Using a cotton bud and a tiny amount of blue paint, fill in the bridges in the centre of each flower. Leave the paint to dry and then fix according to the manufacturer's instructions.

SPRINKLED SHAMROCK TABLECLOTH

This project was inspired by a pattern we recently designed, featuring the much-abused shamrock motif. We found an antique spongeware bowl with this basic idea and then transformed it to make it feel a bit more contemporary. The soft colours of the ceramics sat so well on the natural linen tablecloth, we couldn't resist extending the pattern onto the fabric.

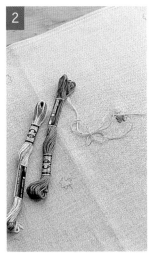

MATERIALS

- *enlarged photocopy of the shamrock template given on page 139*
- *137cm (54in) square natural linen tablecloth*
- *dressmaker's carbon paper*
- *ink pen*
- *dressmaker's pins*
- *2 skeins stranded embroidery thread in shaded green*
- *2 skeins stranded embroidery thread in dark leaf green*
- *embroidery needle*
- *scissors*

1 Ensure that the edges of the photocopied shamrock template are square. Mark the sides of the photocopy with Left, Right, Top and Bottom. This will help you keep the repeats correct. Transfer the outlines to the linen by placing the carbon paper beneath the template and lightly drawing over the top of each image. Start at the top left-hand corner of the cloth and work across the width, matching the corners and edges. Mark the bottom of the first row with pins to give the baseline for the next row. When the first set of repeats is complete, move back to the left-hand side and begin again. It is easier to transfer all the repeats in one session to avoid distortion.

2 Using three strands of embroidery thread as one and using alternate shades, complete each shamrock using satin stitch *(as shown in the diagram on page 139)*. Ensure that each motif is random in colour and that there are not too many of one shade in any one area.

3 To finish, iron the cloth using temperature as indicated for the fabric you have used.

weaving. Quality was built up by importing seed, providing training and new looms, and the promotion of the resulting material was accomplished by being proudly worn and recommended by the interested benefactors.

The Duke of Ormonde even set up a workshop of Dutch linen producers in Carrick on Suir, not too far away from where I live today, so the south of Ireland was certainly included in these efforts to create a linen industry. One of my family's mills was created in 1843 as a flax-scutching mill, all the way down in County Kilkenny. Flax did not grow well in the area, however, and so it was transformed into the flourmill it is today.

When export duties were removed from textile imports in 1700, the linen trade changed from a small, family-style craft into a bigger and bigger business. Small handcrafting operations became larger, setting up mills to use waterpower, or specializing in one efficient operation, such as scutching or weaving. Suddenly, as in all political decisions, export to Britain and the colonies was opened up and demand exploded. Capital flowed into the business

on a serious scale from this stage on and, at every chance, improvements and mergers ensured bigger output. Although, by the beginning of the nineteenth century, many small weaver-farmers still produced linen, the thin end of the wedge was firmly in the door and the wonderful homespun linens that we cherish so highly today were soon to become a thing of the past. By 1825, finely spun thread could be successfully woven on a mechanical loom and factories began to expand into industries, pulling weavers away from their homes and into the cities.

The countryside did not lose all these handcraft skills, however. The very finest linen, used for handkerchiefs, was still being produced by hand weaving: it was the only suitable technique for this finest of fine stuff. Also carried through the years were the traditions of needle craft on linen, especially important after the famine and brought to great prominence in the highly embroidered Victorian era. So country people continued to manufacture the famous Irish linen; it would have been part of their lives and their homes.

Every family here has a little bottom cupboard drawer full of heirloom fabrics, handed down from grandmother or beyond. In Ireland, more often than not these small treasures are made of linen. By the end of the nineteenth century, sewing schools were established throughout Ireland to promote this penny-earning craft among the women of the countryside. The thousands of women who spent their lives embroidering linen, sprigging it, or tatting its edges have left a legacy, and for the large part they were country women, working on a piecework system to help the family economy. How natural that they would keep the odd piece or teach their children the skills. Drawn work was associated with linen and the north, while various forms of cotton embroidery and lacework were developed in areas in the south.

The qualities of linen as a fabric have remained true even in this last gasp of the twentieth century. It can be pure gauze or an impenetrable mass, it is

OPPOSITE

The ubiquitous and perfect Irish linen tea towel, as popular and useful now as it was hundreds of years ago. Here it sits on an old wooden carpenter's chair.

strong and breathes as your body breathes. You can print on it, embroider it, pleat it or knit it. Whatever you do, you can count on it for strength and longevity and functionality, three attributes which certainly make it a venerable component of the Irish country style.

WOOL AND WOVEN TEXTILES

The sheep and the countryman have travelled down a very long road together in Ireland. A multitude of stunningly beautiful wool textiles are being created now and it is a pleasure to say that what is made today is the high point of a craft story that began in the mists of time, hundreds of years ago. Not unlike linen, wool fabrics have had their ups and downs and their regional strengths and weaknesses, but their strength today owes more of its success to the tenacity of the rural dweller than do the highly exported linen products of old. Early examples in the National Museum of plaid costumes made in the Viking era reveal very strong beginnings: fabrics that we would admire today if we saw them worn by friends walking towards us down the street.

West of Ireland tweed is justly famous and originally was spun and woven in remote cottages, often terrifyingly far from the marketplace where it would be brought for sale. In an historical perspective, while the linen trade was booming because of a lifting of an export ban, wool trade and manufacture plummeted as it was prohibited from export at the same time. So wool weaving continued much longer as a cottage industry, as people needed to make their own garments. Only in the twentieth century has tweed production largely become mechanized and achieved the status of a world-wide export industry.

Where there are sheep there are mountains and most of the wonderful tweeds and woven woollens come from these regions. Counties Donegal, Mayo, Galway and Kerry have a long tradition of producing beautiful woollens. The basics of the craft of weaving are identical throughout the country and

TWEED THROW

This throw can be
made very quickly,
especially if the
tweed that you use
frays easily.

WARP *refers to long*
threads in length of fabric.
WEFT *refers to shorter*
threads in the width of
the fabric.

MATERIALS

- *piece of heavy herringbone tweed 2.3 x 1.5m (2½yd x 60in)*
- *ruler or tape*
- *dressmaker's pins*
- *sharp scissors*
- *plywood board measuring 50cm (18in) square*
- *strong drawing pins*
- *clothes pegs*
- *7 shades of double knitting and tweed mixture yarns (1 ball of each)*
- *piece of heavy card measuring 33 x 12cm (13 x 4½in)*
- *rug hook*

1 Straighten each end of your tweed by cutting across the width following one of the threads. Then at one end of the fabric, measure 18cm *(7in)* into the length of the cloth with the ruler and mark with dressmaker's pins right across the width. Fray the loose weft threads as far as the dressmaker's pin and end of cut, until you have an 18cm *(7in)* fringe right across the width of the fabric. Remove the pins and repeat at the other end of the fabric.

2 Attach the woven edge to the corner of the plywood board with drawing pins, allowing the fringe to fall over the edge (work sitting at a table). Then divide the fringe into equal, manageable bunches and further divide into three sections each. Plait quite tightly. Temporarily secure the ends of the plaits with clothes pegs and then whip (bind and tie) each plait with contrasting yarns. Continue across both widths, keeping the plaits even. Carefully trim the ends to neaten.

3 To make multi-coloured plaits, take six strands of knitting yarn in different colour combinations. Wind around the heavy card guide several times. Cut at one end.

4 Use the rug hook and take bunches of six yarns and pull through the tweed between the fringe plaits and 3cm *(1¼in)* up from the edge of the tweed, making a loop and complete with a rug knot. Repeat this at intervals and then plait the bunches of yarn, dividing each group of 12 threads into three. Whip the ends as previously. Repeat at each end of the throw, using as many different colours as you wish.

BELOW AND OPPOSITE

Alice Roden creates unique, intricate woven fabrics in a variety of materials, often working to commission or in very small batches. Her work is for the connoisseur and combines visual simplicity with a truly complex craftsmanship. Here are four samples of her wool weaving made from classical techniques that have withstood the test of time.

vary only in the small details of production. The little animals roaming the mountainsides, which donate the material for this industry on an annual basis, do make a difference to the final feeling and look of the piece. There exist over fifty breeds of sheep and each has a particular virtue or vice associated with its fleece, and blends of different breeds can produce amazing wools.

Colour in its finest, subtlest form is added to the wool at fleece stage. Plant and lichen dyes were used from early days until the twentieth century, when huge demand necessitated commercial colorants being used; there was not enough of the beautiful but slow-growing lichen in Donegal to make the required product. Colours from vegetable matter varied from batch to batch by necessity and several small batches of fleeces dyed the 'same' colour invariably ended up with tiny differences and a mottled effect.

HOMESPUN YARN

To spin your yarn, you must break up your fleece into smaller bits before you wash it. Dry it carefully and pick through the fluff to remove any little nasties or brambly pieces. You may then smear the fibres with fat – preferably goose

fat, but rancid butter will do – then it will be time to card the wool. Two leather-covered pats studded with tiny metal teeth or pins are the carders and the wool is combed between these two pats back and forth to straighten the fibres. The wool is now ready to be spun, so place all your nice little bunches of carded fleece beside you ready to be gathered up with one hand and fed to the spindle in your other hand. As the spindle twists, so it pulls the carefully fed fibres, twisting them into a yarn. At the final stage of spindle's spin, it is important to gather a new batch of wool and carefully twist it into the yarn you have just created.

If you use a spinning wheel and live in County Mayo, you may need to stand to use your big wheel apparatus. If you live in County Kerry, you may sit, as you use a smaller wheel and a low chair will do very well. In Donegal, the 6,000 or so flax spinning wheels distributed in 1796 have ensured that you are inclined to use this sort of spinning wheel, which has a treadle to keep the wheel going round. In any of these regions, but especially in Donegal, spinning was a communal occupation, with the village girls getting together in a special place to pass the evening, carding and spinning and gossiping.

Alice Roden's exquisite woven panel, featuring plain fabric against complex patterns. Simple, but with tremendous detail and colour combinations, this piece presents the highest perfection of the weaver's art. Opposite are piles of dyed wool that are just waiting to be transformed at Philip Cushen's woollen mills.

Homespun yarn gives the most fascinating texture to knitted goods, and although originally not used for the home, knitting has quickly expanded to become synonymous with Ireland. Aran knits, a true product of a few creative women on the Aran Islands many years back, have become such a world-wide success story, that their style has found its way into rugs, carpets, even spreads – any part of a home where complicated simplicity is desirable. Still drawing on these original handcrafting techniques, Kitty Joyce runs a shop called Cleo in Dublin, begun by her mother in 1936. Her devotion to true vernacular style has been unwavering and the quality and colour of the designs she

produces today suggest all the subtle beauties of lichen and berry dyes used long ago. She has a wonderful band of merry knitters whose skill will never be matched by computers or machines.

To create the flecks so typical and so loved in tweed, you will need to put a plain layer of carded wool bundles on the floor. Then, scissor-snip coloured or dyed bits of wool and scatter them over the first layer. Add another plain layer and then more 'bits', whatever colours you desire or have to hand. While spinning, these small fluffs are incorporated into the yarn, resulting in the complex, multi-coloured look associated with good tweed. Just as in pottery or any handcraft, after all this effort there is always more to do – quite a bit more. After creating a seemingly unending supply of yarn, a web can be woven on the loom.

In the last few hundred years, men have been the weavers in Ireland. Looms of very ancient times were only 56cm *(22in)* wide and, indeed, some of the finest hand-woven tweeds of today are only made in such width, but market demands of the nineteenth century insisted on wider production. The main point of creating cloth on a loom is regularity and evenness of the weave and quality control went hand-in-hand with the growth of the industry. Whatever loom was used, perfection was important and formed the base foundation for the cloth. The heddles lifted and fell, alternating the warp strings, while reeds kept the distances between the threads equal. In handloom work, four basic types of pattern were used: tabby is the name for the 'under one, over one' basic weave, while twill is 'under one, over two'. Herringbone and birdseye are the two other types of pattern, still going strong today.

When completely woven, the piece – or web – of cloth is washed again, then rolled onto a bolt while damp to remove creases. After a time, it would be unrolled and then the final character of the piece created. Weaving is only the foundation, much as throwing a pot on a wheel is the foundation of

OPPOSITE

Many Irish weavers still spin their own yarn. This Foxford rug of the Irish national colours was presented to Michael Collins many years ago by the same company. Some things never go out of style in Ireland.

pottery. Surface alteration can vary the texture, feel, and even use of the wool. For example, 'fulling' can take place next, when the wool is boiled and shrunk, then beaten into a slight (or not so slight) felt. The fibres are loosened and interlock more closely with each other, creating a barrier to the outside world. As a supreme example, my wife gave me a pair of Aran islander tweed trousers from O'Maille's in Galway when we were first married. The fabric was as solid as the thickest canvas, and nothing would even think of attacking such wonderful wool. They were made from true Aran tweed and, if I hadn't grown widely into the mellowness of age, they would still be in perfect condition.

Across the hill from where I live, Philip Cushen still creates woven wool fabrics from scratch in his old mill in Graiguenamanagh. Sheep dot the hillsides around and Philip is a master of their by-product; he still spins his own yarns for knitting and weaves myriad blankets, throws, scarves and lengths on his old family looms. Another wonderful Irish textile firm is Kerry Woollen Mills in County Kerry, the home of the horse blanket that has come to stand for simple, fine country cloth. Foxford in County Mayo, started by nuns in the nineteenth century to relieve rural poverty, is still visitable and is a good place to get a feeling for the history of woollens in Ireland.

QUILTS

From the late eighteenth century on, quilts were produced by all social classes in all areas in Ireland. It did not take long for the ever-practical Irish housewife to realise the beauty of recycling cast-off petticoats or bedding and fashioning a brand new, beautiful item to warm the family. Utilitarian, but with a creative freedom few other household objects allowed, quilts today show us the cheerful and strong character of their makers. They were never intended to be sold and were created for immediate use or as heirloom presents for marriageable daughters, so any idea of conformity was abandoned or ignored. That said, most quilts were created in three main ways.

Appliqué This technique uses motifs cut from one print sewn onto another layer of cloth. Very elaborate appliqué quilts survive from the great houses of the eighteenth century, but anyone lucky enough to possess a wonderful piece of coloured printed fabric could undertake this mode. A central large motif would be surrounded with elaborately pieced borders in matching styles of fabric, a bit like the plasterwork being created in that early period. A sort of frame would be formed. In the south, this style degenerated into sewing one

OPPOSITE AND OVERLEAF
Fringing is an integral part of Irish woollens, whether on old shawls or contemporary throws. It is a simple decorative device successfully used to enhance these plain, luxuriously soft scarves made from lambswool. Overleaf, a quilt demonstrates how the brilliant reds of old petticoats were recycled into high art forms in Ulster. After a hard, wet day, imagine the warm welcome that this beautiful bed would provide.

type of fabric onto another. In the north, large patterns of white and red became the most usual survivor. The red petticoats worn by many women enjoyed an extended life when they were combined with bleached and turned flour bags to become highly typical Irish quilts.

Log Cabin This technique was brought from the USA, as far as we know, and is well known all over the quilting world. It entails sewing together rectangular strips of cloth to form a larger square around a small central square. Light and dark strips emanate, like with like, either in conjoining corners, or on opposite sides. The separate units of these dark and light strips can then be put together in astounding combinations. The scale of the work can be altered as well, with some of my favourite quilts being enormous blowups of this idea: one huge central square and then rectangular strips of any and all description, moving outwards.

Mosaic This is what patchwork is most commonly associated with, as it is created by joining squares of identical designs, which have been created by even smaller, geometric units being sewn together. It is a bit of a jigsaw, as all the tiny borders of all the tiny pieces must fit perfectly for the quilt to lie flat. Hexagons, triangles or squares form blocks of pattern, which may then be bordered, or not. Sometimes, the complexity of such methods is thrown out of the window altogethe, and long strips of alternating colours are sewn together, decorated further with only small tufts of cotton protruding from the simplified field.

Quilt making The actual making of a quilt involved sewing together the fancy top and a backing layer, often with padding or bumpf in the middle, and often with a design for the stitching to follow. Pure white fabrics were

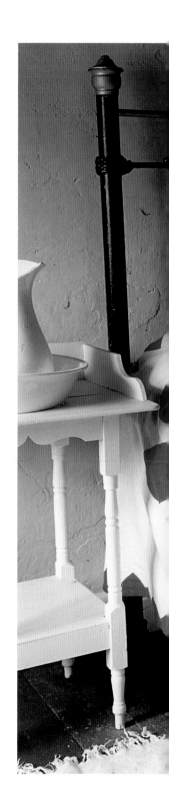

RIGHT

Any colour combinations are possible when you make your own quilt. These contemporary pieces were specially commissioned from Sue Norton in County Cork to blend into this calm, pale interior.

sometimes used, joined by spectacularly rich joining stitches. Candlewick was a technique where threads were stitched closely together in a clump and then released into puffs of texture with a cut of the scissors. It would have been part of pure quilting. The social pleasures of sharing this task with neighbours was a common occurrence in Ireland, as it would have been in the States or anywhere else. It is easier for two or more to assist with the large, unwieldy pieces of cloth and if a quilting frame is used, a partner can push back your needle instantly.

The usefulness of quilts was as important as their beauty and the surviving examples of earlier work show, for the most part, that they were indeed used. The fabric content, both in diversity and in quality and type, reveals much of the history of the quilt, and Ireland continues to present us with a wide-ranging span of types, from the lowest to the highest. Each quilt has its own inimitable – and timeless – charm.

COTTON

Although never grown in Ireland, cotton has become part of the Irish textile repertoire. All the skills associated with linen and tweed were, in time, applied to cotton thread, especially in the last half of the nineteenth century. Irish lace was born at this time, and, when the actual market for lace disappeared, it gradually evolved into what we today call crochet and its related techniques.

Crochet was a true vernacular craft, as it was made both for the home and for personal use. Although it was not strictly a highly sought-after export product, it is still possible to find stunning white bedspreads of heirloom quality, made with crocheted cotton squares, pieced together and then perhaps edged with the famous zigzag. In the beginning, crochet was a poor relation to lace and linen sprigging, but now it has come down to us as a vibrant technique, full of texture and interest.

PATCHWORK QUILT

This quilt design has been plucked from a bit of history. Twenty or so years ago, a well-researched and fascinating exhibition of original Irish quilts was put on by Kilkenny Design Workshops, the semi-state body set up to promote design in Ireland. This quilt is typically pure and simple, both in effect and in the making, and so we offer it here as a bit of Irish style that will be fast and easy to make.

 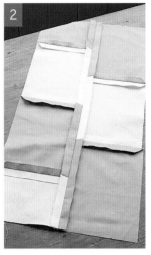  

MATERIALS

- *fabrics (see page 134)*
- *sewing threads in cream and red to match fabric*
- *1.5mm (¹⁄₁₆in) thick card for templates*
- *sewing machine*
- *craft knife*
- *set square*
- *ruler*
- *tape*
- *scissors*
- *sewing needle*
- *dressmaker's pins*
- *iron*

The finished patchwork measures approximately 1.78 x 2.3m (70 x 80in)

Preparation Instructions for making templates and cutting out are given on page 134 with a graph.

1 Cut each patch with a craft knife, using the template. Always lay it on the fabric so the grain of the fabric goes in the same direction. Cut:
80 cream full blocks
8 cream half blocks
9 green full blocks
10 green half blocks.
Following the graph on page 134, stitch together alternate blocks of colour along their short sides to make long strips. Discreetly mark the top block of each strip with

letter A, B, C, etc, to match the graph. Clip each seam and press.

2 With right sides facing, stitch strip A to strip B, and B to C down each length until all are joined according to the graph. Iron well, trim the ends if uneven and press seams open. With right sides facing, join the edge strips to the patchwork sides *(see graph)*, trim and iron.

3 Cut the interlining to the size of the patchwork. Lay out and place the quilt on top, wrong side down. Join together 6mm (¹⁄₂in) in from the edge. Make a

backing from the red fabric measuring 1.70 x 1.82m *(67 x 72in)*, joining fabric if necessary. Join the cream backing strips to each side of the red backing. Pin the backing to the interlining and stitch all together with a 6mm *(¹⁄₄in)* seam.

4 For side bindings, fold each in half lengthwise, and fold in the raw edges by 13mm *(¹⁄₂in)*. Pin over the edge of each side and slip stitch in place. Repeat for the end bindings. Neaten the end seams. Press well and spot quilt *(see page 135)* for extra embellishment.

SHEEP CUSHION PANEL

This little sheep belongs to our range of pottery called 'Landscape.' Among all the animals we feature on this range, he is one of the most loved, so we have moved him onto this little cushion cover to make him even cuddlier.

MATERIALS

- *30cm (12in) square of linen union fabric*
- *fine permanent black pen*
- *acetate*
- *Sheep Cushion templates (pages 136–7)*
- *craft knife and cutting mat*
- *masking tape*
- *dressmaker's carbon paper*
- *piece of plywood 50cm (18in) square*
- *sponges*
- *cotton thread in white*
- *ready-made cushion cover and pad measuring 50cm (18in) square*
- *fabric paints in blue, white, green, brown and black*
- *embroidery thread in green and brown*

Preparation Tape the square of linen union in the centre of the plywood board, using masking tape. Using a set square and ruler, draw a 25cm *(10in)* square in the centre of the fabric with dressmaker's chalk. Using the carbon paper and template photocopy, transfer the dotted square into the centre of the marked square. This is a location marker for the stencils and an embroidery line, so make sure it is clear. Enlarge the outlines on pages 136-7 as marked. Transfer the six numbered outlines to acetate and cut out with the craft knife.

1 Position the first stencil with masking tape. Mix blue and white paints on the plate for sky blue and apply with the sponge, graduating and blending in some pure white for cloud effect. Leave to dry. With a mixture of green and white, paint stencil 2.

2 Paint through stencils 3, 4 and 5, following the key on page 136 for the right colours. Let colours dry between stencils.

3 Before using stencil 6, use the sheep's wool guide from page 136 to mark the embroidery positions. Use the black marker pen

and press the point firmly through the acetate. For the sheep's features, use the remaining stencil and black paint. Remove stencil and then follow the manufacturer's instructions to fix the colours.

4 Use brown thread to work chain stitch *(see page 136)* on top of the innermost dotted line. Cut out 25cm *(10in)* from the 30cm *(12in)* square and turn under a 1cm *(½in)* seam allowance all around and neaten the corners. Sew onto the centre of the cushion and use bullion stitch *(see page 136)* to make the fleece.

CHAPTER 4

FURNITURE

Country furniture in Ireland possesses its own naïve charm and even after many years, I find myself still smitten. I love the crazy individualism of each piece, the textures of use and the touches of decoration. Stemming from the same medieval furnishing traditions as in Wales, the basic pieces in a cottage evolved into the open dresser, the settle, chests and built-in beds and cupboards. In use, all were arranged in a comfortably rigid pattern, depending on the layout of the main kitchen area. The most visually elaborate object was the dresser, resplendent with layers of Delft and tin and bits and pieces. Next down the visual hierarchy was the settle, then tables and the wide and ever-changing variety of seats and chairs.

Small three-legged stools called creepies and chairs with seats of roped straw called sugan chairs are particularly Irish. Pine, ash and sycamore were the commonest woods used, as they were the cheapest and most easily obtained. The actual pieces made and used settled into a well-defined functional tradition early on, with references in the seventeenth century to objects which were still in use in the twentieth century. This long time span of tried and true rural objects speaks volumes for the utility and purposefulness of the furniture that country dwellers employed. If something works, don't change it; if it still looks all right, don't buy another. Similarly, the arrangement of furniture was preordained and rarely altered – the dresser stood opposite the hearth, the settle on the far wall, the table against the wall and the many stools, chairs and benches moved freely, often finding themselves outside on a fine day.

FURNITURE FOR SITTING ON AND DINING OFF

Irish chairs are most irresistible to me, probably because they are so redolent of life and usage. There were various types of plain wooden chair and to me the most fascinating are what today's antique dealers incorrectly call 'famine' chairs. In reality these chairs were fashioned from hedgerow materials and cheaply gathered bits of wood and were made totally from wood. A thick solid plank for a seat was most usual, with angled, gently carved sticks added for legs and arms and backs. For a curve, the actual shape of the piece of wood determined the angle of the top seat back, as early carpenters would not have had elaborate steaming processes to hand. These chairs are natural style at its best, unselfconsciously using different types of wood in combination. The makers would have taken the owner's leg and back size into consideration as well, so customization was the rule of the day back then. Although primitive is the description most often applied, their bare minimalism links many of

OPPOSITE AND LEFT

Opposite are two typical Irish chairs. The one on the left has a recently made string seat and the chair itself has a typical minimalist block cutting to the back and legs. That on the right is an old armchair, which would originally have had a straw or sugan seat. The thin spindles on the back are typical of pole lathe turning. The traditional Irish kitchen to the left is filled with plain shapes that contrast strongly with each other and no effort has been made to disguise or pretend.

them to our own modern aesthetic. And their designs are so varied and so individualistic, it is difficult to pin them down to a region or specific maker. They were made well into the early twentieth century and have inspired at least one modern craftsman to keep the tradition alive. One thing they all seem to possess is a slightly wild, happy quality.

Stools Wee stools were even more commonplace than stick chairs, three-legged ones more commonplace than four-legged 'creepies'. These totally portable, almost anonymous bits of furniture were made low to the ground to protect the fireside dwellers from the smoky draughts of the open-hearth chimney. In early drawings or prints of Irish life long ago, the fireside gatherings depicted arranged themselves on many angles, with the majority quite close to the floor (the guest of honour sat closest to the fire). Again the seat would have been made from a single slab of wood, with legs angled in. Three legs withstood the vicissitudes of stone floors more easily than four and their size allowed them to be stored beneath or on top of other pieces of furniture if the dancers needed more room.

Sugan chairs These grace many old pubs in Ireland still and were made up until very recently. They are made from straw gathered from the field, twisted or spun out of a haystack and the technique relies on tight turning to hold it together. A seatless chair of wood with stretchers between the legs provided the framework on which the ropes of straw were strung, side to side, then back to front. The twentieth-century examples are mostly rough in shape and square cut, although earlier lathe-turned and shaped-back examples can be found. The finished product produces a warm, comfortable seat that can be repaired easily and which costs almost nothing. When first made, a sugan chair behaves like a moulting dog, leaving bits of straw here and there, but

OPPOSITE

A little painted table fashioned from hedgerow sticks and continuing the tradition of rustic furniture until very recently. Tables such as this are lightweight, portable and serviceable, and are appropriately called 'gypsy' tables.

after some use it settles into being a well-behaved member of any interior. I remember seeing sugan being made in the fields after haymaking, and it appeared almost magically, with one neighbour walking away from the stack of hay while another pulled and gathered the bits to be twisted. Sugan was used for almost any purpose – as handy as a bit of string and, unlike its modern alternatives, totally recyclable! It died out when plastic string and rope became commonplace in local shops, as it could never compete with the eternal lifespan of the brilliantly coloured usurpers.

Carpenters' chairs Paint was often applied to the wooden frames of sugan chairs, just as it was for a slightly grander type of seat known as 'carpenters' chairs'. These were wooden sabre-legged chairs derived from an original Regency style of chair, produced and in widespread use long after the Regency style had died out. These little wooden seats required extra skill and machinery and were probably produced on a small batch scale in Ireland. Since they were made from pine, they were invariably painted. Only mahogany and oak escaped the paintbrush, as they were destined for the 'parlour'. Our ancestors would have been horrified to allow cheap wood to be seen naked in their homes, and stripped pine would have caused total apoplexy. Only the seats of benches, certain chairs and tables were kept free of paint, as they were continually sand scrubbed for hygienic reasons.

Settles Other seating was provided by settles; these were armed benches with draught-proofing backs, either panelled or slatted, which could, at a pinch, provide a sleeping platform for the weary traveller. To ensure a restful night's sleep, they were made with a deep seat which compromised the daytime comfort of anyone without the longest legs. They were made in all shapes and sizes, to suit a particular room or need, and often were the most well

crafted piece of furniture in the house. Settle beds take the idea further, with a box bed suddenly springing to life when the seat of the bench is folded down. These were often heirloom pieces in Irish families, and so created with flair and untypical decorative touches. Elaborate panelling and mouldings were applied to back and arms, especially in the region I live in (County Kilkenny). The beds so formed were multi-purpose as well; they could hide any amount of household bedding, they could safely contain a drunken guest or a curious child or two or three, and often did. Not famous for comfort, they were most often used for visitors or small children. Our modern equivalent is the sofa bed, although you couldn't rest a crock of milk on a sofa bed.

Benches Another double use, super-efficient type of furniture 'invented' by the Irish was a bench or 'form' hinged to the wall. It was usually allied with a table similarly hinged and both could be lowered or raised. There were even table tops attached to settle benches; these acted as backs to the settle but could be pulled up and laid over the bench to provide a large, strong table. This nifty idea even extended to individual chairs, too: chair-tables. So one part of Irish country style is efficiency through invention.

Forms were a mainstay of early interiors and were the simplest type of strong, long bench, with solid ends for legs. A form could seat three or four, it could be moved easily and it could be found outside the front door to welcome passers-by to drop by for a bit of gossip. They could also serve as tables or workstands. Indeed, their universal usefulness made sure they were included in every household and they are still visible (and useful) today.

Tables Similarly basic were tables. In Ireland, these were almost always rectangular as they would be pushed back against the kitchen wall when not required for eating. The tops needed to be as thick and strong as possible

OPPOSITE

Here is an authentic old Irish creepie ready to scuttle away. We just happened to come across it when taking the photographs for this book and felt that it was just too good to miss.

and the bases needed long cross stretchers to provide storage for dairy crocks as well as feet. A drawer would not go amiss and most examples surviving today do have a cutlery drawer or two on either the long side or short. The basic feeling was sturdy, strong and square timbered. Also they were painted on the legs only, so that the sanding and cleaning could be carried out on top. The variation in design across Ireland does not seem strong and little evidence of the individuality found in stick chairs can be found in old tables nowadays. There is, however, a classic quality about these objects, which, when tempered with years of shaping by wear and tear, renders them also irresistible.

AROUND THE HOME

The last half of the nineteenth century saw brand-new, bought-in pieces of furniture joining the basic and homemade items made over the centuries previously. A Victorian style crept into the parlours or 'rooms' of better-off Irish country dwellings, adding a formal layer over the earlier, easy-going

OPPOSITE AND BELOW

The door opposite, worn through touch and use, opens onto the kitchen. The settle below — otherwise known as a high-backed bench — has simple back panels and arm details. It is handsome enough to make anyone sit up straight.

RIGHT

Although contemporary,
the pure forms of this Irish
bedroom connect strongly
with the simple shapes
and colours of the past.
The bed was made, and
belongs to Sacha Whelan,
a furniture maker in
County Cork.

style. As these rooms were only used for very set occasions, like a visit by the priest or doctor or other elevated personage, they do not seem to have altered the basic atmosphere of an Irish country cottage. To me, these rooms were always strangely removed and, if I dare say so, an amazing waste of space, but their use as a buffer against out of the ordinary occurrences is intriguing and many cultures share this need. In Ireland, elaborately turned Victorian tables, sideboards and upholstered settees were gathered into the parlour, along with bits of crystal and brass and pictures. Often these rooms were so fusty and musty and unused, the worst thing to have happen when visiting would be to get led into the parlour!

In the bedroom Sleeping arrangements in the old days depended on how large the cottage was and how many people needed to sleep. Various regional differences did occur, with outcrops clinging onto the side of the house or more elaborate 'west rooms' being used for sleep. Beds were found in lofts above the hearth, in gable end rooms and even right next to the hearth. The most charming beds were created in alcoves, with decorated woodwork and hanging drapes. These were snuggled into a nook or pitched roof and insulated with fabrics and sometimes wallpaper. Straw matting (sometimes just straw) and big feathery mattresses kept the sleepers warm. With the advent of industrially produced iron bedsteads, these simpler forms of bed were overtaken by the curvilinear look of iron. With a galleried washstand, a blanket chest and heirloom quilt, the quintessential Irish bedroom look was completed.

In the kitchen Back down in the kitchen, dressers, of course, are the high point of Irish country life: when they are good, they are great and when they are bad they are still good. But other cupboards were also used in Ireland as well as dressers. Food cupboards were enclosed, four-door affairs, often with

MUG RACK

This simple Irish mug rack comes from my mother's collection and usually sits in her tiny spongeware museum. It is such an easy but charming project I could not think of anything better to reproduce. The zigs and zags are primitive and forceful and the main form of decoration.

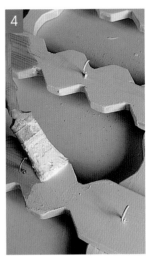

MATERIALS

- *3 pieces 2.5 x 10cm (1 x 4in) pine measuring 87.5cm (34½in) – horizontal bars*
- *3 pieces 2.5 x 7.5cm (1 x 3in) pine measuring 65cm (25½in) – vertical bars*
- *templates from page 139 transferred onto card and cut to size*
- *saw*
- *small clamps*
- *sscrews*
- *cup hooks*
- *sandpaper*
- *drill*
- *matt varnish*
- *white spirit*

1 On the horizontal bars, use a pencil and the corner template to draw the points for the ends. Draw as heavily as you like: it will be painted over. Then, with the horizontal notch template, draw at each end and on each side, notches about 15cm (6in) from the end, wider side facing out. Leaving a straight space of 2.5cm (1in) on both sides, make two more notches. Leaving another 2.5cm (1in) gap, make two more pairs of notches, pointing to centre.
You should have a 10cm (4in) gap in the centre with three pairs of notches regularly emanating out to

the end on both sides of the wood.
Repeat for the shorter lengths of wood, using the vertical notch template. Begin the pairs of notches about 18cm (7in) from the ends. For each corner, use the vertical corner template to create right angles.

2 Using the saw, cut out all the notches to make zigzag shapes. Sand lightly on the cut edges.

3 Lay out the vertical pieces and place the horizontals on top, so the longer, un-notched sections of the verticals line up with the longer centre and

end sections of the horizontals. Drill two starter holes into the centre of each conjoining section and then carefully screw them together. Clamps would come in handy here.

4 Mark where you want to put cup hooks. Then drill and screw them in. Prime the wood, undercoat it and apply the final coat. If using in a kitchen, it is worth sealing the final coat with a matt varnish to protect it from atmospheric damage. Some black or dark brown pigment added to your varnish will help to age it.

two drawers in the middle. These were large, almost ungainly pieces of furniture but held a good amount of comestibles. Mug racks, meal bins, salt boxes and a wide array of candleholders and other tiny shelf units completed the kitchen furniture. Simply crafted from crossed planks of wood, mug racks featured protruding hooks of wood or iron on which to hang everyday cups. They were often decorated with chamfering and, occasionally, other motifs. Salt boxes, knife boxes and candleholders were created in all shapes and sizes, sometimes with mirrors, sometimes with fretwork, sometimes with only a bit of paint. Their obligatory coat of paint would have contributed to any colouring in the interior.

Paint allows matt textures to be created as well as glossy and they can be readily combined too. Interior walls of cottages were often painted in two tones; the most common arrangement being cream and green, with green enamel on the bottom bit of a wall and matt cream distemper on the top half. This shiny and matt surfacing allowed easier cleaning and also the shiny surface reflected any ambient light from a window or fire. The matt emulsion top half could be repainted more often, at less expense, so it presented a saving as well. What I like about it today is its extraordinary cosiness. Another particularly Irish design was the use of quite simple R&V sheeting panelling going half way up a room, all the way around it. Much like plain painted old cream and green, this panelling would have been painted or scumbled to contrast with the remaining wall; concealing the great Irish problem of rising damp and probably providing a bit of insulation at the same time.

IRISH DRESSERS

Irish dressers were solid, one-piece affairs, not like the Welsh version at all. They started off open, and incorporated an enormous variety of design possibilities, depending on what a particular household needed or used or

LEFT

Here is a dresser that is

dripping with a small

jumble of our own pots.

They all glitter cosily

together in the firelight.

Plain or painted, these individualistic wall boxes could keep a variety of necessities to hand. These boxes were commonplace throughout Ireland and can still be found in antique shops in fair number. The variety of shape and size is as limitless as the imagination of the makers.

wanted to show off. The dresser was certainly the most decorative object in an Irish cottage, as it would be dripping with pottery and Delft and bits of tin and china, glittering cosily in the firelight.

If I were to create my own dresser tomorrow (something I would love to do), I would take a careful look at the space in my kitchen. I would also gather up all the things I think I might put on the dresser and take a good hard look at them, with a view to presenting them at their best. Deciding what you need and then having it made is certainly the traditional way to go when acquiring an Irish dresser and was the deciding factor in all designs of earlier days. Getting the local handyman to knock up what you want is not so easy nowadays (getting a handyman period is not so easy), but careful searches of antique shops and furniture outlets may provide the right size and shape for your dream object. The shelves of the dream dresser should ideally suit your favourite domestic objects; as I have more mugs and bowls than larger pieces, I would have at least four small shelves to display them and leave one shelf for plates and one for platters. If I can manage a few nesting hens, I shall leave the bottom open for hatching sites.

DECORATING THE DRESSER

Colour – both dark and light shades – was so important in Irish kitchens that it was frequently applied to other surfaces: most especially the dresser. When an array of industrial paints hit the Irish market in the late nineteenth century, no colour was left untried. This choice was entirely personal. A new bride coming into a home could express her own preferences by changing the colour and the display of a dresser. Very often, two-tone dressers were created, with panelling picked out in contrasting colours, or with larger flat areas stippled or wildly brush-marked in contrast to surrounding areas. Dressers give you a chance to go a bit wild.

False wood-graining techniques were often employed, by laying a thin, oily surface of paint over a glossy underlay, and then combing textures and patterns into the top film. Other, more three-dimensional, decorations also found their way onto dressers and I have a little list of some of my favourites. These would have been part of the actual woodwork, incised or cut out of it, or added onto it. An all-covering coat of paint would have ensured their felicitous union with the piece itself and so, even today, we could certainly personalize a plain bought-in dresser with any of these motifs.

Sunbursts Rays of wood radiating from a central point can compose a very dynamic look. They are not the easiest of motifs to create, as they require careful tapering from centre to circumference and must be closely set together to be effective, but when done properly, they look magnificent.

Reeding Reeding usually indicates tiny, straight cuts running parallel and very close together, like a bundle of reeds. It creates a texture with subtle light-catching properties and quietly enlivens a straight stretch of wood.

Cross-hatching Diagonal cross-hatching with a saw on the uprights of the dresser created interest and a richness to match more sophisticated ornamentation. A file or a chisel could similarly create a cross-hatch pattern.

Hearts, diamonds, clubs and spades These symbols appear almost anywhere, gouged out of the tops of humble dressers and in the most elaborate, big house shelves: they are universally appealing.

Dentil moulding The relief of cube and moulding alternating was especially popular. A derivative of the big house ceiling, dentils are lively and delicate at the same time and help pull the top cornice and shelves below into unity.

BUYING FURNITURE

Many old iron bedsteads can still be purchased today, as indeed can many other types and pieces of early Irish antique furniture, although much of it has sadly been exported over the years. My parents helped to found a little group which called itself the Irish Country Furniture Society. About twenty

FROM LEFT TO RIGHT
A three-dimensional zigzag pyramid; simply gouged roundels on an old blanket chest; a sunburst or fan for enlivening the corner of a panel, and cut-out hearts and diamonds, which were extremely popular. Wood was added to, carved or cut out in the most basic ways to create pleasing decorations.

years ago, they travelled all over the country in an effort to save some good examples of Irish furniture, but even at that time they were sorry to see how much had been exported. The society gathered together a charming group of pieces, which can now be seen in the Johnstown Agricultural Centre, just outside Wexford. Although now it is difficult to track down such excellent examples, there is still a brisk market in vernacular furniture and the list of antique dealers at the end of the book may help you if you want to search. By constantly seeking, ye shall find.

When buying stick chairs, the important point to remember is to look for all-wood pieces, without nails or screws. Dressers are priced by the degree of ornamentation or quality of wood in the piece; the merrier it is, the more it is. And, as in all antique purchasing, it is important to look out for fakes and reproductions. It is always best to go to dealers with a high reputation who have an idea of provenance. Original paint is always desirable, as are the wee marks of wear and tear which have shaped a piece over the years. Perhaps because of the very primitive nature of much of early Irish furniture, I am happy to say it is still affordable for the keen collector.

For a contemporary version of traditional Irish furniture, it is interesting to find new craftsmen returning to the style in increasing numbers. Eric Connor has been working successfully from Dublin for a number of years and his designs are drawn directly from vernacular Irish furniture, but using finer woods and true wood finishes. Sacha Whelan, down in Shanagarry in County Cork, creates pieces of wonderfully simple elegance, using a great variety of native hardwoods . He manages to keep the earlier proportions of Irish country furniture, while sensitively combining them with modern touches and materials. The pieces Sacha Whelan creates are timeless and could fit into any decorating scheme, and their beautiful handmade quality and finish make them welcome well and truly anywhere.

LEFT

A large, unpainted chest
sits in front of a window
whose only adornments are
shutters painted white and
a collection of plants.
The combination is one
of rural simplicity.

SMALL SCUMBLED CUPBOARD

This project is a surface-changing technique, aimed at 'improving' the look of something. For colour and feeling, I have based it on some wildly scumbled doors in a butcher's shop in Gort, County Galway, long since painted over. The technique just involves laying scumbling oil over a slick surface of paint and combing through and was a popular trick in Ireland.

MATERIALS

- *high gloss paint*
- *scumbling oil or gloss paint*
- *brush*
- *combs*
- *prepared board on which to test your ideas*
- *absorbent rags*
- *white spirits*

1 Paint the cupboard with a coat of undercoat.

2 Lay a good layer of high gloss paint over the entire surface of the cupboard. On large areas, brush carefully in one direction and as smoothly as you are able. Allow to dry well. Decide what design you want to do by making a small sketch of the cupboard with the desired final effects. With light pencil marks, transfer roughly what you have decided to do onto the gloss paint surface.

3 Working in sections, brush on the top coat of scumbling oil. This should be rather light, as the combing will condense the surface paint into stronger lines. If you thin the oil slightly it will work well. When the layer has started to stiffen a bit, use the comb to create the effects you desire.

4 For the combs, use either a professional plastic paint one or cut your own from flexible plastic, such as a dough scraper or from a rubber window-cleaning squeegee. I found a paste scraper ideal for the job as it has a handle. The spacing of the tiny notches will greatly affect the final outcome. Try to keep the comb at the same angle as you work, and make sure it doesn't get too full of excess paint. Wipe away excess as you go. Twirls are created by rotating the comb on one axis. Straight parallel lines of combing require careful but simply drawn straight combing. It is a good idea to practise a bit first on your test area. Work on a side or section of the piece at a time. If you don't like what you have done, remove the scumbling oil with a cloth while still wet. When finished, allow to dry well.

CHAPTER 5

ELEMENTS

Baskets have been with us since the beginning and I suspect they will be there at the end. There is no real substitute for a good strong basket: lightweight, flexible, comfortable to use, recyclable, made from sustainable harvests and visually appealing to boot. Any farmyard need imaginable can be satisfied by making a suitable basket. No doubt because the basic material for Irish baskets – the sally or salix – grows here in fifty or so varieties and grows well and quickly, Irish baskets were part of everyday life in every country dwelling. From Neolithic times on, they have been important tools of toil. They were made in a multitude of shapes, as form followed function so carefully. The shallow, circular skibs and potato baskets have a very specific Irish quality to them and seem to me to be the most typical style. The basic size of these corresponded to the length of a man's arm from elbow to fingertip, as the outer frame of rods had to be held in one arm during fabrication. A good basket maker could make about thirty skibs a day, if properly organized with well-prepared rods and materials.

These small baskets could take potatoes from the field or the clamp and then, when the taties are boiled, hold them over the pot to steam, waiting patiently for the family to gather round to eat them. If the dogs didn't get the peelings, the basket could be used to flick out the remains to the waiting hens. It might then be ready and clean to carry washing in from the line. There is not much that such a shape cannot do. Much larger sally baskets were produced for holding or carrying turf; the little donkey creels and the large, round, straight-sided baskets of 1m *(3ft)* or more are good examples of early functional design. The basic skill of basket making was a common part and parcel of everyone's life, although gradually, more specialist basket makers evolved and made containers on a small industrial scale. These would have been for sale in markets throughout Ireland in any shape or size and were certainly affordable.

Fishing and all its related activity required a fascinating amount of paraphernalia, and basket weave was often utilized to great effect. Even though they date back to at least medieval times, eel traps are still useful objects if you have the proper licence. Traps or creels specifically shaped for crab or lobster were commonplace until recently, and a superior type of trap was made from heather. What could be more lightweight than baskets to take with you in the boat? Baskets of all types were created for all types of fish and fishermen. Even boats were made from wicker rods formed into large shallow baskets and covered with softened cowhide. I remember these treacherous little bubble boats as being the poacher's best friend; easy to hide, easy to carry, easy to escape notice. Two would be used in tandem to net salmon.

Traditional baskets for domestic use carry on even today. One man in particular, Joe Shanahan, was the third-generation son of basket makers and, until he died, trained many young men in the craft down in Carrick on Suir, where he lived. There was not a lot Joe did not know about baskets. He and my father and I all went to New York together back in the early 1980s, to show the world what Irish craft was all about. Joe was absolutely wonderful and beguiled what seemed like all the sophisticated ladies of New York with his charm and skill and story telling. For a long period, he made baskets for Sybil Connolly for her more discerning customers. I remember one amusing phone call where Sybil desperately needed a basket large enough to hold a St Bernard dog for a client in America. Joe merely pulled a design for a hot air balloon basket from his memory and set to work – quite a world away from his earlier productions of potato and turf baskets.

Beautiful, simple, serious Irish baskets can still be found today, although they seem to be scarcer now than ten years ago. Joe Hogan in Connemara works from home and his 0.5 hectare *(1 acre)* sally garden provides him with enough rods to produce exquisite baskets. Another young basket maker who

Two products of the earth:
a sugan chair with its
seat made from straw rope
and a carry all made
from rushes. Both are still
around today.

'grows his own' down in Cork is Norbert Platz. He and Louise Tollman have been making baskets for fifteen years, and although they find much of their inspiration in the old-style baskets from the west of Ireland. They also create wonderful contemporary designs – not to mention scarecrows!

Rush work is another Irish craft that has survived until today. A much softer material than sally, rushes are harvested along riverbanks and estuaries and then carefully stacked and dried over a two-month period. To work and weave the rushes, they must first be flattened and then wetted again. The particular golden green colour of objects made from rushes is wonderfully

inimitable and for small-scale items it is an unbeatable natural material, with a distinctively Irish flavour. Mats, baskets, bags and beautiful boxes made in this way are all still available in Ireland.

GLASS

Glass is not something the average country dweller can whip up from local ingredients in the back yard. A good source of silica sand and fluxes, plus a limitless supply of wood for the furnace might have helped nurture some sort of early glass industry in Ireland, but for whatever reasons, it never developed into a common commodity. When the indigenous forests were cut down in the late sixteenth century to fuel the forges of English industry, there were 'forest' glass houses that followed the woodsmen. These very early invading craftsmen would have used the fuel that came to hand, in the true Irish tradition. It wasn't until 1670 that a finer quality glass house was set up at Lazar's Hill in Dublin, near where Trinity College is today. The main flowering of Irish glass had to wait until the next century, however, when glassmakers were allowed Free Trade, and so able to compete with English merchants, unfettered in the marketplace. Much like the linen trade that grew so rapidly at this time, small glass houses increased their skills, efficiency and production and many glassblowers came to Ireland from England to make their fortune.

What happened then was similar to what happened to the wool trade. Little by little, punitive tariffs were introduced as the glass trade was perceived as a threat to English industry. It didn't happen overnight and many Irish glassmakers struggled along into the late nineteenth century. Waterford glass, in its earlier manifestation, began in the exuberant glassmaking period in 1783; by 1851, it gave up and went out of business. Many other glassmakers, such as those in Cork and Belfast, suffered the same fate and disappeared. By 1890, the last flint glass house in Ireland had closed its doors in Dublin.

OPPOSITE

Varying types of sally or willow create different colours in the finished product. The shapes vary too – here are round and rectangular baskets that can be used to hold a wide variety of items.

121

What was actually made by these Irish glassmakers in the hundred or so years of their existence is fascinating to me today. The features I admire most in this simple, early glass are the colour and the fast, simple blowing used to produce it. Obviously, for a true country style, deep surface cutting would be an abomination (death of a thousand cuts) and I shall leave that entire branch of well-established Irish glass in the parlour where it belongs. Although a small amount of grand glass was produced by some Irish glassmakers in the early years, intense English competition and domination in this top end of the market forced a majority of Irish glassmakers to stay simple and less elaborate. The eighteenth-century style of flat cut surface decoration, a technique which uses manually powered wheels to grind the surface into patterns, went on in Ireland much longer than elsewhere. The gentle, almost primitive look of this technique is a far cry from the deeply cut English ware. Indeed, eighteenth-century designs continued well into the nineteenth.

Another technique I admire was one using moulded flutes – these tiny undulations were blown out into a mould and the hot glass would have been pushed up against the carved ripples in forming the piece. These early Irish glass pieces have that simple, sympathetic, idiosyncratic feel about them that allows them brotherhood in the family of Irish country objects.

From the 1820s to the 1840s, when Irish glassmaking suffered fairly insurmountable trade difficulties, many glass workshops became smaller – similar in scale to what we would consider studios today. The glass these workshops produced was so simple, handblown, so spontaneous, that it looks as if it were produced yesterday by a sophisticated glassblower. These pieces were produced quickly and cheaply, often using colour, and would have been destined for a local buying public. This is the period of Irish glassmaking that reveals the maker's hand. These lesser-known examples of what I admire in Irish glass are closer to the true, humbler style of simplicity of form and

OPPOSITE

Here is a small collection of mouthblown glassware from Belfast, made around 1820. These simple and sympathetic colours were added to a hot glass mixture to camouflage impurities in the mix.

125

function. The material speaks for itself and quite eloquently. Glasses and jugs were blown straight up or into wooden moulds. Stems were either very plain, or punctuated with simple discs between body and stem and foot. Throughout the glass itself, swirls and tiny imperfections betray the hand of the maker and give us an idea of the time spent in the making. You can almost feel the hot glass rising and twirling into place under the calm eye of the glassblower.

I live near one of Ireland's main hot glassblowing workshops, Jerpoint Glass, and have always admired their plain, straightforward approach to design. Keith Leadbetter, who used to work with Simon Pearce when he lived in Ireland (Simon is now a major glassblower in the USA), started up Jerpoint with his wife Kathleen in 1979. Jerpoint Glass now produces a variety of simple, robust stemware that has a true Irish country feel to it. Keith works in the middle of the countryside, surrounded by fields and flowers and animals, and the five teams of people he has trained to work with him are from the

OPPOSITE AND BELOW

This beautiful Irish corner cupboard holds a fine collection of early Irish and English glassware. Two examples are shown below: a harp has been etched onto an early nineteenth-century piece with moulded fluting, and on the right there is more fluting and a shallow cutting of Irish origin.

local area. When Keith started up, he remembers that elderly local farmers came to buy his glass, as it reminded them of what they used when growing up. At that time, they felt it was too 'plain' and undecorated to present to others as a gift, so they just bought it for themselves – a true testimony to the country-style simplicity of his glass. Using one of Keith's glasses is like shaking his hand – there is a warmth only a handmade object possesses.

WOODTURNING

Since prehistory, all sorts of wooden containers were cut and then hand-carved from solid timber. Heavy but beautiful bowls, drinking vessels known as methers – a form of square wooden mug with handles – and even churns now seen only in museums were often carved from bog oak, the 'pickled' wood that has lain preserved in the tannic acid of bogs for thousands of years. In the intervening years, wood has continued to serve the Irish country dweller and, aside from vessels, other carved items in common use included butter boards, butter stamps, yokes for cattle, spoons and tools.

Until quite recent times, the great majority of domestic wood ware used in the country districts and in small towns was produced by local woodturners. The most-used lathe during the nineteenth century was the pole lathe – a simple, portable machine that was quite adequate for the making of utility items. There are earlier tales of famous turners who could make enormous bowls just by using a pole lathe. Again, as in other crafts, the utmost simplicity accompanied the creation of wide butter bowls, ladles, potato beatles. These early implements can still be found in antique shops and their use as accessories in our own homes today can lend a curious twist or look to a room. The woodturner also helped provide the local handyman/carpenter with decorative spindles for chair backs, dressers or sets of stairs. Whatever wood was to hand was used, ash and sycamore being more desirable than pine.

OPPOSITE

These lovingly created handcarved spoons were made by Neil Foulkes in County Laois. They are resting in a simple wooden bowl that has been turned on a pole lathe. The only ornamentation is a small engraved band on the outside of the bowl.

Today, the woodturning craftworker concentrates on making very fine individual pieces for a far more affluent market. He (or she) would be equipped with an electric lathe, a wide range of special chisels and many different abrasives and chemicals for finishing and polishing. The wood used is no longer gathered by the wayside, but obtained from importers, although some woodturners do gather and store their own supplies of wood, often finding fallen, diseased hardwood trees which will produce the most startling results on the lathe. My brother Keith is a woodturner and he used to hunt for huge unwanted baulks of dead trees and leave them around to dry for a good while. Like pole lathe turners before him, he especially loves making large vessels of beautifully simple shape, letting the complexity of the aged material form the intricate surface detail. The natural qualities of wood connect these contemporary pieces with their forebears and, as before, the simplest shapes often work the best.

Of today's professional woodturners, Liam O'Neill and Roger Bennett produce beautiful pieces. Liam works on a very large scale and his shapes range from simple to elaborate. The figuring of the wood almost always plays a major part in his work. Roger Bennett is the other side of the coin. His work is intimately scaled and he imbues his grain with soft, lustrous stains. Although contemporary in look, its simplicity allows it into the Irish tradition.

RUSTIC FURNITURE

Another use of wood common in the Irish countryside was the fabrication of rustic furniture. Although it grew out of another tradition, it has been part of the Irish scene since the eighteenth century. It had no true link to peasant culture except conceptually and was the by-product of the aristocracy's longing for a simpler life. When forests and woods were being developed on large estates, the thinnings and leftovers were often turned into objects of rough,

OPPOSITE AND LEFT

Sticks and vines can be shaped and twisted into myriad shapes and all manner of furniture created for both the garden and inside the home.

bark-covered simplicity. Sticks and lumps and vines and roots were deemed curious and suitable building materials for the creation of gates, chairs, benches, screens and tables to use in the gardens of the rich.

When we moved to our present little house (a woodsman's cottage) in the middle of the woods, we found ourselves in the middle of just such an estate forest, where planting had been an important industry in the eighteenth century. We also found ourselves the owners of a secret, hidden garden dating from 1790, complete with waterfall and ruined cottage orne. From drawings of the time, the romance of what we were living on top of entranced us and we set about restoring this lost little Romantic period garden. One of the most wonderful things about the early drawings we found were the rustic seats and benches and building details, using branches and twigs and vines.

To us it was essential to bring back this early style of furniture. The totally modern use of natural materials and extremely abstract look of the objects was an amusing coincidence and some of the very early drawings of Irish branch furniture would look perfect in one of today's better art galleries. The idea of bringing a piece of 'true' tree into a house is romantically comforting.

As we were reconstructing the cottage, I had to learn the techniques of 200 years ago. Rustic furniture was derived from the hedgerow as well as from under thinnings. Ash, hazel and the odd bit of honeysuckle are the main ingredients we used for our rustic revivals. All grow readily nearby and are indigenous plants that replenish themselves easily. Frames can be concocted from thick, straight branches of ash trees. Split, straight-growing hazel rods can then be tacked onto the frame, flat side down, in a variety of styles.

This rustic style does belong to the Irish countryside, as the tradition continued during the Victorian era. It was similarly popular in England and the continent and spread to the United States too; today, instead of being a rarefied style belonging to few, it is enjoyed by many.

OPPOSITE

Twigs, branches and underthinnings can all be used to create anything from fences to seats to tables. These are from our garden, Kilfane Glen, near Thomastown.

PATCHWORK QUILT

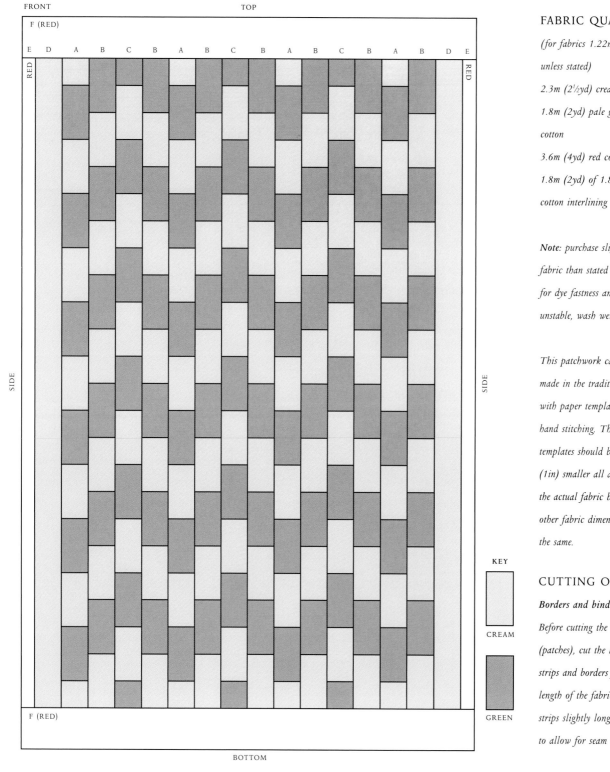

FABRIC QUANTITIES

(for fabrics 1.22m [48in] wide unless stated)

2.3m (2½yd) cream cotton

1.8m (2yd) pale green glazed cotton

3.6m (4yd) red cotton poplin

1.8m (2yd) of 1.8m (70in) wide cotton interlining

Note*: purchase slightly more fabric than stated and wash test for dye fastness and shrinkage. If unstable, wash well and iron.*

This patchwork can also be made in the traditional manner with paper templates and by hand stitching. The paper templates should be cut 25mm (1in) smaller all around than the actual fabric blocks. All other fabric dimensions remain the same.

KEY

CREAM

GREEN

CUTTING OUT

Borders and bindings

Before cutting the blocks (patches), cut the longer side strips and borders from the length of the fabrics. Cut these strips slightly longer than stated to allow for seam discrepancies.

BROWN JUG AND BIRD PLATE

Front edge strips

2 cream: 16.5cm x 1.82m

(6½ x 72in)

Backing strips

2 cream: 5cm x 1.82m

(2 x 72in)

Side bindings

2 red: 7.5cm x 1.82m

(3 x 72in)

End bindings

2 red: 20cm x 1.85m

(8 x 73in)

TEMPLATES

Cut two templates from the thick card using the ruler and set square to make sure the blocks are accurate.

Full block:

12.5 x 17.5cm (5 x 7in)

Half block:

12.5 x 10cm (5 x 4in)

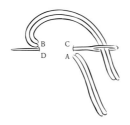

SPOT QUILTING STITCH

Thread needle with two heavy strands of mercerized cotton. Put needle through at point A and leave 50mm (2in) of thread hanging. Emerge at B and reinsert at C. Emerge at D, pull through and cut the thread to 50mm (2in).

RIGHT AND BELOW RIGHT

The two templates required for the Brown Jug projects (see pages 36-7). Transfer onto separate pieces of acetate.

BELOW

The Bird Plate templates (see pages 52-3). Transfer the birds onto one piece of acetate and the branches onto another.

135

SHEEP CUSHION

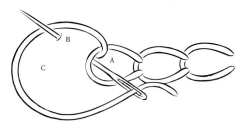

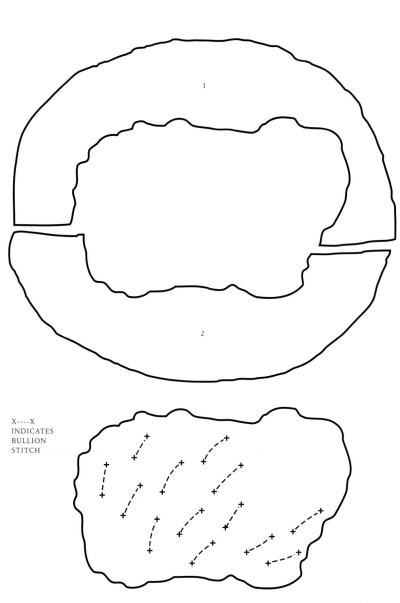

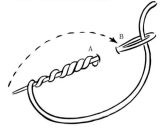

Chain stitch

Bring thread through at A. Lay the thread in a loop, holding it down with left thumb. Reinsert again at A and bring it through at B. If making a straight chain, bring it through at C. Bringing it through at B will turn a corner.

ABOVE

Bullion stitch

Bring thread through at A and reinsert at B. Bring needle point only at A again. Do not pull through. Twist the thread around the needle until there is enough wound onto cover the space between A and B. Holding the twists carefully with the left hand, draw the thread and needle gently through. Take the thread in reverse, pulling back to B. Reinsert needle at B and either move onto next stitch or fasten off.

X----X
INDICATES
BULLION
STITCH

SHEEP'S WOOL GUIDE

TOP AND ABOVE

The six templates for the Sheep Cushion Panel project (pages 84-5). Enlarge the outlines to twice the size on a photocopier and then transfer to acetate as described on page 85.

STENCIL
PAINTING KEY

1 *Slate grey blue + white*

2 *Leaf green + white*

3 *Leaf green*

4 *Havana brown*

5 *Slate grey blue*

6 *Black*

CHAIN STITCH

CHAIN STITCH

STENCILLED CURTAINS AND SHAMROCK BOWL

TOP

50% REDUCTION FROM ORIGINAL TO SHOW HOW TO POSITION ON A4 ACETATE

LEFT AND BELOW

Using a black felt-tipped pen, transfer the stencil outline given below twice onto a piece of A4 acetate, positioning the flowers as given in the diagram to the left. Repeat with the second piece of A4 acetate and then return to the preparation instructions given on page 59.

100% SIZE

SHAMROCK BOWL MOTIFS

CLUSTER

SINGLE

STEM/TWIG

LEFT

The three templates required for the Shamrock Bowl projects (see pages 42-3). Transfer onto separate pieces of acetate.

SHAMROCK TABLECLOTH AND MUG RACK

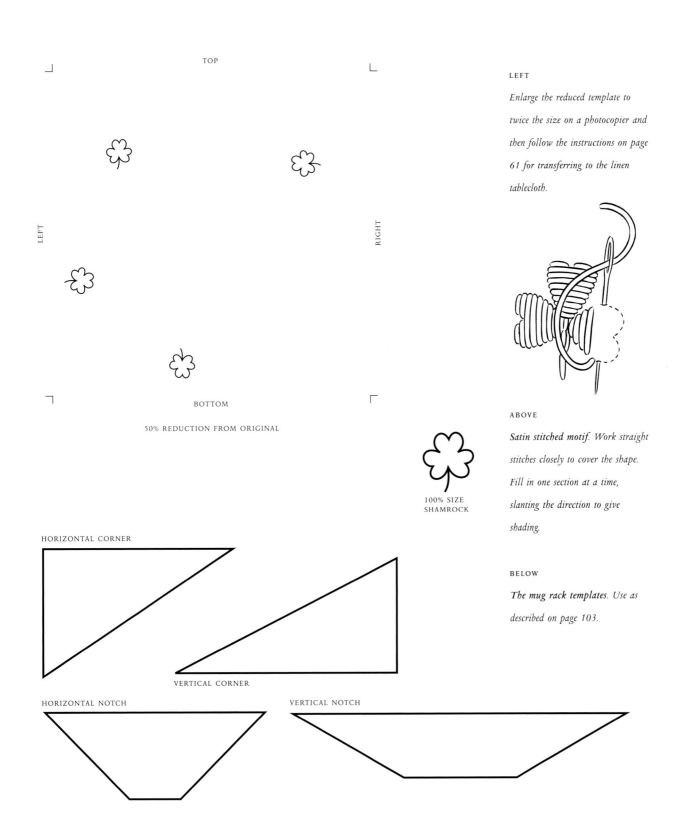

TOP

LEFT

RIGHT

BOTTOM

50% REDUCTION FROM ORIGINAL

HORIZONTAL CORNER

VERTICAL CORNER

HORIZONTAL NOTCH

VERTICAL NOTCH

100% SIZE
SHAMROCK

LEFT

Enlarge the reduced template to twice the size on a photocopier and then follow the instructions on page 61 for transferring to the linen tablecloth.

ABOVE

Satin stitched motif. *Work straight stitches closely to cover the shape. Fill in one section at a time, slanting the direction to give shading.*

BELOW

The mug rack templates. *Use as described on page 103.*

ANTIQUE DEALERS

These Irish antique dealers carry stock that changes frequently. If you are specific in what you are looking for, phone before going.

Agar Antiques
92 Main Street, Saintfield
Tel: 01238 511214

Attic Antiques
90 Main Street, Saintfield
Tel: 01238 511057

Ballinderry Antiques
Wesley Mills, Ballinderry Upper,
Nr Lisburn
Tel: 01846 651046

Ballindullagh Barn
Killadeas,, Enniskillen
Tel: 01365621548

Ballyalton Architectural Co.
39 Ballyrainey Road,
Newtownards
Tel: 01247 813235

Bartlett's Bazaar
Bridge Street, Ringsend
Dublin
Tel: 01 6602182

Beaufield Mews Antiques
Woodlands Avenue
Stillorgan
Tel: 01 2880375

Blackthorn Antiques
2 Meetinghouse Street,
Donaghadee
Tel: 01247 882642

Bob Christie Antiques
20 Calhame Road, Straid,
Ballyclare
Tel: 01960 341149

Clarinbridge Antiques
Clarinbridge, Galway
Tel: 091 796522

Country Interiors
42 Upper Abbeygate Street,
Galway
Tel: 091 562799

Delaney Antiques
Cork Road, Newport
Tel: 061 378180

Fox's Corner Market
4 London Street, Londonderry
Tel: 01504 371551

Goodwood Pine Furniture
Rosebank, Old Blackrock Road,
Cork, Co. Cork
Tel: 021 318418

Honan's Antiques
Crowe Street, Gort
Tel: 091 31407

Tony Honan Antiques
14 Abbey Street, Ennis
Tel: 065 28137

Satch Kiely Antiques
The Quay, Westport
Tel: 098 24775

Kenyon Antiques
9 Great Strand St & 10 Lr
Ormond Quay, Dublin
Tel: 01 8730625

Mill Court Antiques
99 Lurgan Road, Seapatrick,
Banbridge
Tel: 018206 62909

Moy Antiques
12 The Square, Moy
Tel: 01868 784895

Now & Then Antiques
51 Bridge Street, Lisburn
Tel: 01846 605879

O'Keefe's Antiques
15 Prince's Street, Tralee
Tel: 066 25635

Quilligan's Antiques
Main Street, Adare, Co. Limerick
Tel: 061 396515

George Stacpoole
Main Street, Adare, Co. Limerick
Tel: 061 396409
Fax: 061 396733

Terrace Antiques
441A Lisburn Road, Belfast
Tel: 01232 663943

CRAFT SHOPS

These shops feature the contemporary crafts featured in this book. Each shop will have its own particular stock and look, so phone in advance if you are looking for any specific product.

Avoca Handweavers*
Kilmacanougue, Bray, Co.
Wicklow
Tel: 01 2867466

Ballymaloe Craftshop*
Shanagarry, Co. Cork
Tel: 021 652032

Bay Tree*
118 High Street, Holywood,
Co. Down
Tel: 0801 232 426414

Blarney Woollen Mills*
Blarney, Co. Cork
Tel: 021 385280

Boland's Craftshop*
Boland, Kinsale, Co. Cork
Tel: 021 772161

Cleo Ltd
18 Kildare Street, Dublin
Tel: 201 6761421

Crane Bag Gallery*
15 Broughshane St. Ballymena
Tel: 0801 26640569

Craftworks*
Bedford House, Bedford St.,
Belfast BT2 8AA
Tel: 01232 244465

Design Options*
Hynds Lane, Portlaoise,
Co. Laois
Tel: 0502 60688

Doolin Craft Gallery*
Doolin, Co. Clare
Tel: 065 74309

Instore Accessories*
Todds Bow, Cruises Street,
Limerick
Tel: 061 416608

Kilkenny Design Centre*
Castle Yard
Kilkenny
Tel: 056 22118

Kilkenny Shop*
Nassau St, Dublin
Tel: 01 6777066

Magee & Co
The Diamond, Donegal Town,
Tel: 073 71100

National Museum
Kildare Street & Merrion
Square, Dublin
Tel: 01 6777444

Quinlan's Pottery Shop*
New Street, Macroom, Co. Cork
Tel: 026 41198

Treasure Chest*
William St. Galway, Co. Galway
Tel: 091 563862

Tuckmill Crafts*
Dublin Road, Naas, Co. Kildare
Tel: 045 879761

Ulster Weavers*
34 Factory Store,
Mountgomery Road,
Belfast BT6 Q22
Tel: 0801 23204236

Whitethorn*
Ballyvaughan,
Co. Clare
Tel: 065 77044

* Shops that supply Nicholas Mosse pottery (see also opposite)

CRAFTSPEOPLE

These are only a few of the people who produce handmade objects in Ireland and they are either people we know or whose work we particularly admire. For further information, the Crafts Council of Ireland will be happy to answer queries about general crafts or more specific requests. For such a small country, there is a wealth of craft people and product.

CERAMICS

Tania Mosse and Alex Dufort
Brixton Pottery, 9 Harper's Lane, Presteigne, Powys, LD8 2AN, UK
Tel: 01544 260577

Paddy Murphy Pottery
Enniscorthy, Co. Wexford
Tel: 054 35443

Michael Roche
Kiltrea Bridge Pottery, Caim, Co. Wexford
Tel: 054 35107

FURNITURE

Gabriel Casey
Cahermakeria, Lisdoonvarna, Co. Clare
Tel: 065 747668

Eric Connor
The Studio, 18 Bath Street, Dublin 4
Tel: 01 2352787

Lynn Kirkham
Bohernarudda, Killea, Templemore, Co. Offal
Tel: 0504 32341

Clive Nunn
Ballyduff Mill, Thomastown, Co. Kilkenny
Tel: 056 58473

Sacha Whelan
Ballycotton, Co. Cork,
Tel: 021 652149

Neil Foulkes
Miskaun,
Aughnasheelin,
Ballinamore,
Co. Leitrim
Tel: 078 44765

GLASS

Jerpoint Glass
Stoneyford, Co. Kilkenny
Tel: 056 24350

RUSHWORK & BASKETS

Patricia O'Flaherty
Cloonshee, Strokestown, Co. Roscommon
Tel: 075 37077

Norbert Platz
Ballymurphy,
Innishannon,
Co. Cork
Tel: 021 885548

Patricia d'Arcy, Basketry Museum
Mount Nugent,
Co. Cavan
Tel: 049 40179

Joe Hogan
Loch na Fooey, Finny,
Clonbur,
Co. Galway
Tel: 092 48241

Barbara-Ja Kelly
Poulfur, Fethard-on-Sea,
New Ross,
Co. Wexford
Tel: 051 397240

Lynn Kirkham
Bohernarudda, Killea,
Templemore, Co. Offaly
Tel: 0504 32341

TEXTILES & PATCHWORK

Alice Roden
Clonlea, Church Hill,
Enniskerry,
Co. Wicklow
Tel: 01 2829679

Ferguson's Irish Linen
54 Scarva Rd., Banbridge, Co Down
BT32 3AU
Tel: 018206 23491

Kitty Joyce
Cleo, 18 Kildare Street, Dublin 2
Tel: 01 652032

Jennifer Trigwell
Textile Designs,
Brownstown,
Kilkenny
Tel: 056 22937

Susan Norton
Kilcor, Castlelyons,
Co. Cork
Tel: 021 652032

Philip Cushen
Cushendale Woollen Mills,
Graiguenamanagh,
Co. Kilkenny
Tel: 0503 24118

WOODTURNING

Roger Bennett
Carrick, Castlejordan,
Tullamore, Co. Offaly
Tel: 01 4922224

Liam O'Neill
Spiddal Craft Centre,
Spiddal,
Co. Galway
Tel: 091 553633

Ciaran Forbes
Glenstal Abbey, Murroe,
Co. Limerick
Tel: 061 386103

Neil Foulkes
Miskaun,
Aughnasheelin,
Ballinamore,
Co. Leitrim
Tel: 078 44765

NICHOLAS MOSSE POTTERY

For Nicholas Mosse Pottery stockists, any of the starred shops in the Craft Shop list above would have a selection of the range, although there are many more shops in Ireland and the UK that stock the pottery. Those carrying the greatest stock would be Ballymaloe Craft Shop in Cork and The Kilkenny Shop in Dublin. For more information, mail order or wholesale requests, please contact us directly:

Nicholas Mosse Pottery
Bennettsbridge
Co. Kilkenny
Tel: 056 27105
Fax: 056 27491
www: NicholasMosse.com

ACKNOWLEDGMENTS

I have had the pleasure of being surrounded by keen enthusiasts during the making of this book. **Denise Bates** started the whole thing off, my wife **Susan** held my hand while writing, and **Jennifer Trigwell** was a supreme collaborator on all the textile designs, projects and object gathering. **Debbie Patterson** was the fastest, most sympathetic photographer, and **Tessa Evelegh** kept us all organized. My mother **Elizabeth** generously offered access to her collection of Irish goodies and patiently watched it all disappear and reappear, time and again. **Wendy and Sacha Whelan** in Cork and **Kitty Joyce** in Dublin also gave unstintingly in the cause of showing off Irish crafts. **Peter Francis** helped me enormously with his unerring sense of history and style.

Looking back over the history of vernacular crafts in Ireland, I think there are some perceptible influences that kept rural craft alive and kicking and allowed it to flourish as it does today. From the days of a beneficent government agency called the Congested Districts Board, created in 1891, concern for local living conditions gradually evolved onto individual members of society. **Muriel Gahan** was one of these, and perhaps the most forceful of all. In her later, and my earlier, years I met her when she was head of the Crafts Council of Ireland, where her astute intelligence and brilliant support for all crafts were evident. Over her long life, her love of homespuns, real baskets, rushwork and all things Irish never wavered and influenced a generation.

Her work, often motivated by charitable impulses, was carried on by the setting up of the **Kilkenny Design Workshops** and the formation and incorporation of the **Crafts Council of Ireland**. Both these bodies set to work assisting and improving Irish crafts in a bid to create real and viable business in the countryside. Like Muriel Gahan, they also did their best to promote visual design in the widest sense, and 100 years on, the efforts have been successful. Through these years, people like **Blanaid Reddin** ploughed a way for our idiosyncratic Irish style to survive and become a continuing part of the country's heritage. Our wonderful friend **Sybil Connolly** also spent her life indefatigably promoting craftspeople working in the farthest flung parts of the island. **David Shaw Smith** is another important promoter of rural craft, through his beautiful films and book. There are many people who loved the countryside enough to make a difference: my parents **Elizabeth and Stanley Mosse** were especially important to me. As Ireland goes rapidly spinning into the twenty-first century, I think this is an appropriate time to offer every one of them – wherever they are – a sincere thank you.